ARTICLES OF PEACE

Articles of Peace

Celebrating fifty years of
Peace News

Edited by Gail Chester and Andrew Rigby

PRISM
PRESS

Bridport, Dorset · San Leandro, California

Published in 1986
by PRISM PRESS
2 South Street
Bridport
Dorset, DT6 3NQ

and

PO Box 778
San Leandro
California 94577

ISBN 0 907061 90 7

Printed by The Guernsey Press, Guernsey

Contents

Contributors   xi

Foreword   1

Introduction — *Meg Beresford*   3

Peace News, 1936-1986 — *Andrew Rigby*   7

Pacifism, war resistance, and the struggle against
nuclear weapons
     Part One — *Michael Randle*   27
     Part Two — *Diana Shelley*   36

Non violent resistance and social defence
— *Howard Clark*   49

To live our lives so as to take away the occasion for
war: some observations on the peaceful economy
— *Tom Woodhouse*   70

Be practical, do the impossible: The politics of everyday
life — *Andrew Rigby*   90

Shelter from the storm: under the green umbrella
— *Chris Jones*   106

'Trafalgar Square was packed as tight as a bunny
girl's bra . . .': Women's issues in *Peace News*
— *Lesley Mair*   127

Liberation and development: Gandhian and pacifist
perspectives — *Geoffrey Ostergaard*   142

Afterword — *Petra Kelly*   169

List of Illustrations

Peace News' London office and Housmans Bookshop at 5   p. xiv
Caledonian Road, King's Cross, soon after its purchase in 1959.

Street selling in 1954.   p. 14

Hugh Brock (left), editor from 1955-64, interviewing Commander   p. 18
Albert Bigelow on his way back to the USA from the Delhi-Peking
Friendship March organised by the World Peace Brigade in
1963.

Polaris Action Group, organised by the Direct Action Committee,   p. 34
attempted to obstruct US Polaris submarines on the Holy Loch in
May 1961. A sub and the US supply ship are visible in the
background.

In May 1963 Committee of 100 demonstrators entered RAF   p. 38
Marham in Norfolk to reclaim it for peaceful purposes. Sixty eight
were charged under Section 1 of the Official Secrets Act; solidarity
action a week later, in which a further 56 people were arrested on the
base, led to the substitution of a less serious charge for all of
them.

Demonstrators scaling the fence at Molesworth, proposed second   p. 46
Cruise missile base, in March 1986.

A key function of the Resistance in Europe against Nazi occupation   p. 56
was the dissemination of information. Here a Danish dental clinic
was converted into a composing room; it could be restored at a
moment's notice, with the typesetters becoming the dentist and his
patients.

Nonviolent direct action — a six-month continuous blockade of   p. 64
farmland at Luxulyan in Cornwall — prevented the Central
Electricity Generating Board from conducting test drilling for a
nuclear power station. A 'captive' drilling rig is shown here in June
1981. Eventually the CEGB abandoned its plans for Luxulyan.

Campaigning in Stevenage by the Direct Action Committee in 1959   p. 76
led to a strike and demonstration by building workers for
diversification of local industry.

In 1976 Lucas Aerospace Workers presented their Alternative   p. 82
Corporate Plan, with 150 suggestions for socially useful products.
The bus, which runs either on the road or on rails could extend
public transport economically as well as using the skills of workers
currently employed in the armaments industry.

From 1970 some thousand squatters created the Free Town of   p. 98
Christiana in a 54-acre disused barracks in Copenhagen.

The peace camps of the 1980s continue the tradition of nonviolence p. 103
both as resistance and immediate personal change. One of the
women's peace camps at Greenham Common, July 1985.

Opposition to nuclear power has grown. Here demonstrators p. 111
nonviolently obstruct construction work at the site of Torness
nuclear power station in 1980.

Organising in small groups is a more recent development in the p. 114
peace movement. People who have just been deported from
Denmark during the War Resisters' International Nonviolent March
for Demilitarisation in 1985 greet each other.

Liverpool Women's Peace March, February 1940. p. 132

Chester Women for Peace on one of the Star Marches to Greenham p. 135
Common, 1983.

Gandhi spinning on board the cross channel steamer as he travelled p. 148
to the round table conference in London in 1931.

Everyman III at Gravesend before sailing to Leningrad in 1961. p. 157

To Humphrey and Kathleen Moore, who inspired the founding of *Peace News*, to Harry Mister, a member of that founding group who has worked so hard ever since, and to the memory of Hugh Brock, Editor from 1955 to 1964, who died in 1985.

The Contributors

Gail Chester, born in 1951, bought her first CND badge in 1959 and has always regretted that her orthodox Jewish parents wouldn't let her miss Passover and go to Aldermaston. She has been making up for it since by running Ultra Violet Enterprises, a radical publishing agency which assists projects such as this book, and by being active in the Women's Liberation Movement, especially the Feminism and Nonviolence Society Group. If she had straight hair and could play the guitar, she would like to be Joan Baez. Instead she sings in the Feminist Choir and is learning the trumpet.

Meg Beresford — born in Birmingham, England, 5th September 1937. "My life cycle — like an insect's — has been through several dramatic changes. Farm child, boarding school, service wife and mother, community worker, mature student and peace campaigner. I was a late developer, and life has improved through the changes. In the peace movement, I've been a grass roots campaigner in Oxford; organiser for END; worker in CND as Council member, Vice Chair and lastly as General Secretary. What follows — who knows?"

Michael Randle, born in 1933, was a conscientious objector to conscription, 1952, and a member of Operation Gandhi and Non-Violent Resistance Group in the early 1950s. Member of the Direct Action Committee Against Nuclear War, 1957-61, and Secretary of the Committee of 100, 1960-61. One of six Committee of 100 workers jailed under the Official Secrets Act in 1962 for organising a demonstration at Wethersfield USAF base. Worked on *Peace News* in 1957-58 and 1963, and frequent contributor in 1960s and 1970s. Council member of War Resisters' International. Since 1980, co-ordinator of the Alternative Defence Commission based at the Bradford School of Peace Studies.

Diana Shelley, born in 1943, has worked as a secretary, actor, journalist and historian and is now commissioning editor at CND. She worked on *Peace News* (1975-6) and is a director of Peace News, Peace News Trustees and Housmans Bookshop. Political involvements include the Committee of 100 (1963-4), British Withdrawal from Northern Ireland Campaign (1973-7), squatting and the women's liberation movement. Currently a member of the Feminism and Nonviolence Study Group, the War Resisters' International and the peace movement Legal Support Unit. Publications include *A Legal Advice Pack for Nuclear Disarmers* (CND, 1984).

Howard Clark has been involved in nonviolent action since 1968. He was co-editor of *Peace News* (1971-76) and is author of *Making Nonviolent Revolution* (Peace News, 1977 and 1981), *Atoms for War* (CND, 1982) and co-author of *Preparing for Nonviolent Direct Action* (CND/Peace News, 1984). He is now on the staff of War Resisters' International.

Tom Woodhouse has worked at the School of Peace Studies at Bradford University since 1974. He has written about labour and social history, industrial democracy and arms conversion. He is interested in peace research generally, and in the possibilities of conversion and diversification of defence industries. He is Editor of *Peace Research Reports* and involved with the formation of the Arms Conversion Group which unites the efforts of researchers, activists and trade unionists concerned with the problems of defence industries.

Andrew Rigby is a trustee of *Peace News* and has been a contributor to the paper over the years. He teaches at the School of Peace Studies at the University of Bradford, where he is also a trustee of the Commonweal Collection, and is rumoured to be the treasurer of the local disarmament group. As a smoker, a non-vegetarian and a lover of competitive sports and powerful (British) motorbikes, he wonders whether he was the most appropriate person to contribute a chapter on alternative lifestyles!

Chris Jones was a *Peace News* co-editor from 1976 to 1982, following failed attempts at several careers, including shoe-shop assistant, milling machine operator and service in the Royal Air Force. He now lives with three adults (including two ex-*Peace News* co-editors) and two children on a smallholding where, apart from attempting a more ecologically sound and self-reliant lifestyle, he has become obsessed with playing the double bass in the jazz idiom.

Lesley Mair was born in Scotland in 1950 and first encountered protest on Holy Lock when made to swim in it one April at Guide camp. Since the early 1970s she has been active in both the women's liberation and peace movements and is part of the Feminism and Nonviolence Study Group which published *Shrew, Feminism and Nonviolence* (1978) and *Piecing It Together: Feminism and Nonviolence* (1983). A former coordinator of the Campaign Against Arms Trade, she now works for Amnesty International. She contributed occasionally to *Peace News* under the name Lesley Merryfinch.

Geoffrey Ostergaard teaches politics at Birmingham University and has been a Peace News Trustee since 1975. Of his many publications on the Gandhian movement since Gandhi, the latest is *Nonviolent Revolution in India* (Gandhi Peace Foundation/Housmans, 1985).

Petra Kelly is 38 and a founder member of the Green Party in the Federal Republic of Germany. She was Chairperson of the Green Party (1980-82), speaker for the Green Parliamentary Group (1983-84) and has been a member of the Federal Parliament since 1983, including membership of the Foreign Relations and Disarmament Committee. She has worked as an EEC civil servant in Brussels, with responsibility for health and social affairs. She travels widely lecturing on ecology, feminism, nonviolence, disarmament and social defence. She founded a children's cancer foundation after the death of her sister from cancer.

Peace News' London office and Housmans Bookshop at 5 Caledonian Road, King's Cross, soon after its purchase in 1959.

Foreword

Peace News started publication in June 1936, and has been published continuously ever since, making it one of the oldest radical papers in Britain, probably the world. To celebrate the fifty years of radical pacifist publishing, the Trustees of *Peace News* decided to produce a book which would not merely concentrate on past glories (of which there are many) but would discuss issues relevant to the peace movement that *Peace News* serves today.

The peace movement has changed enormously in the last fifty years, and we have been fortunate to have a magazine that has been flexible enough to change with it. For this reason *Peace News* has remained an essential organising tool for those of us trying to bring about a radical nonviolent transformation of society.

With the world today under constant threat of violent destruction, the importance of pacifist thought and nonviolent action should be obvious. However, too often, pacifism has been presented as a simplistic 'say "no"' to war. This book aims to show that whilst resistance to war and war preparations has remained a significant element of pacifist action, pacifists have also been concerned to restructure the whole social system, in order to eliminate the causes of war and violence which permeate society. The chapters in this book reflect both the history of such ideas and their contemporary relevance.

Looking at the past helps us to evaluate the present critically and so become better equipped to construct a worthwhile future. Pacifists have a vision of that future, although we may differ amongst ourselves regarding the details. But we all believe that change is possible and that we can begin to live some of those changes now. 'Unity in diversity' lies at the heart of the nonviolent approach to change and has also characterised the process of producing this book. We asked each contributor to take a different aspect of nonviolent change, drawing on the material in *Peace News* as well as their own experience. We hope that the chapters combine to strengthen our different visions and help us in our determination to achieve them.

It is thanks to the determination of a few people that this book has been produced. Diana Shelley, representing Peace News Trustees, has been a vital link in guiding the book from Andrew's conception through to Gail's hammering (non-violently, of course!) of the articles into final shape. Without Diana's persistence and assistance the book might not have been published; she also did the picture research, with help from Amanda Tatham. Colin Spooner at Prism Press has been a considerate and helpful publisher. Special thanks should be made to the staff at Friends House Library; the staff of the Commonweal Collection, a peace movement library and archive housed in the University of Bradford; to Harry Mister, Secretary of Peace News Trustees; and to Colette Galza.

Gail Chester
Andrew Rigby
London and Bradford, July 1986

Introduction

by Meg Beresford

I first met *Peace News* the paper and the *Peace News* ideas of
'nonviolent revolution' in the early heady days of Campaign
Atom, in the spring of 1980. The paper, through its articles,
news reports, letter columns, events listings, was and is an
invaluable source of ideas and means of networking. Members
of the *Peace News* collective past and present — Diana Shelley,
Howard Clark, Mike Holderness and others — came to Oxford,
worked with us in our first marches, assisted with workshops on
nonviolence training, listened, talked, shared ideas and supported us. Through *Peace News*, our group discovered the
networks round the country and were linked up with the anti-
nuclear power groups of the 1970s and with newly-established
and existing anti-weapons campaigns. With a history of
pacifism, I found myself catapulted into a whole new network of
personal friendships.

I am a pacifist both by inheritance and by conviction. My
grandfather and father were conscientious objectors in the First
and Second World Wars. My early childhood was spent in a
closed communal environment surrounded by adults who had
chosen not to fight in the Second World War. We farmed, all of
us playing our part. The bombing, blitzes, deaths and suffering
were a background relayed through the worried conversations
of our parents, clustered round the wireless anxiously listening
to the six o'clock news, in letters from my grandmother who
lived in 'bomb alley' in Kent, in the excitement of watching the
petrol gauge of our one car hovering near the empty mark as we
travelled from delivering milk to the hospital — with the
ignition turned off, we coasted downhill, sometimes got out and
pushed on the flat, and never quite believed we'd make it home.

At first we didn't go to school. We had lessons at home,
reading, nature study in the woods, taught by one of the
women. Later, aged about six, after some of my friends had left

the safety of the country to return to London with their parents, I had lessons with another child in the village. Her father was in the army — and it was only then that I became conscious of some difference and discrimination. Why was my father, young and able-bodied, not away fighting? Nothing was said, but I felt the resentment and criticism.

In 1943 we moved from the Forest of Dean to a new and bigger farm in Somerset. We travelled in a ramshackle lorry piled high with bird coops, farm machinery, and milk churns, over the River Severn on the Aust Ferry, through Bristol. It was the first time I'd ever seen a town. Small children playing in the streets pointed at the crates of geese on the lorry back: 'Coo, look at them big ducks,' as we trundled on. My world suddenly expanded. In the sleepy Somerset village, I went to school for the first time. I knew nothing of children's games, was totally unprepared for the sea of unfamiliar faces and felt plummeted into a new and dangerous place. There were two of us from the farm — both rather small for our age and timid. Immediately we became the focus of attention — because our fathers were safe at home. We spent the breaks hiding in the laurel bushes away from the taunts of our class mates. Back at the farm gangs of Italians were brought each day from a prisoner of war camp to hoe the fields and pick up potatoes, then driven home at night.

Looking back, and as a parent myself, it seems extraordinary that no-one talked to us about why they were there farming and not fighting in the war. They were simply too busy, too bound up in the extraordinary difficulties of learning the craft and skills of farming, from scratch.

Of the men, my father was town-bred, university-educated, a writer who had, up to 1939, worked for the BBC. The others had worked in advertising, the law and business. The women were housewives (in the 1930s most middle-class women were) — catapulted into catering meals for twenty or more, working in the fields and milking cows. What kept them together was their religious and moral conviction that conscientious objection was right and that fighting and killing, even to destroy a great evil like Hitler's Nazism, was wrong.

My early years — the war broke out two days after my third birthday — were spent cocooned in this very closed environment. Friends all lived on the farm. School was a daily sortie into the world of the enemy, to be got through until life began again at home. Later I went to a boarding school by the sea in Cornwall and then another in the West Country. I started on a career in farming, working on a mountain farm in Wales and from there to agricultural college. But, inevitably, I reacted wildly against my parents. We had moved by this time to Salisbury Plain. Surrounded by military camps, I went out with soldiers and eventually married a man in the RAF. I was as fascinated by the uniforms and the military as Lydia Bennet in *Pride and Prejudice*. But the fascination faded. I found I was quite unsuited to the life of a service wife. I started to think and read seriously for the first time in my life. Based on an isolated RAF camp, close to the Northumberland coast, I discovered Bertrand Russell, Virginia Woolf, Vera Brittain. From the standpoint of my childhood grounding, I started again to question the role of the army, of militarisation, the nuclear deterrent, and to revert to the received convictions of my childhood. I left my marriage and embarked on a serious course of personal education, through community politics and university, political awakening, feminist consciousness and have come full circle, working for peace in the 1980s.

I feel able to say I am a pacifist by inheritence and by conviction, but have to make some qualifications. Because of my age, my sex, and the political climate of Britain in the 1980s, these convictions have never been put to any kind of test. Had I been a man I would have done national service (I did in a sense, by marrying into the forces). It is easy, comparatively speaking, to condemn violence, to promote active civil disobedience, to translate the teachings of Gandhi and Martin Luther King to our situation at nuclear bases or in central London, when the costs are no higher than a prison sentence or a fine. Within CND and the wider peace movement, pacifism has little cost in human or psychological terms, even given the undoubted privations and harassments of Greenham Common or Cruisewatch. We can get up and go. It is not Crossroads squatter camp, Soweto, Central Belfast, or Beirut.

Like Greens, Christians, or anarchists, pacifists are just another grouping within the larger peace movement. And at one level, the participation, conviction and commitment of pacifists helps to promote active peacemaking: within ourselves, in our relationships with each other and in our movement, and in the way we relate to the outside world. It helps with the acts of reconciliation between ourselves and the police and military, between peace camps and local populations round Molesworth and Greenham Common. And in the imaginative leap we make when we plan our campaign backwards from the utopian disarmed world which is our goal.

But it leaves questions and challenges unanswered. Should we, as peacemakers, be trying to help in other areas of political strife — the miners' strike, Wapping, the inner cities, where violence to and by both sides comes too quickly to the surface? Many of us have been too involved with our own specific objectives to make the necessary links. We have ordered our priorities — nuclear concerns are at the top — so this is where all our efforts go.

I have focused this essay on my early experience, because it taught me some important lessons. There is the danger of the peace movement becoming a closed environment of like-minded people, focused on its own concerns, talking only to ourselves. Like our farm, we are so busy keeping ourselves going that we don't have time or surplus energy to get out and talk to the people who don't agree with us. As things get difficult we turn in on ourselves, get bogged down in the business of running our campaigns as ends in themselves, and lose sight of our aims. Avoiding this must be an important part of our struggle.

Peace News, 1936–1986:
An Overview

Andrew Rigby

Peace News had its origins in a pacifist study group convened by Humphrey Moore in Wood Green, London in 1936. Having completed their programme of studies they decided to engage in some form of practical action that would propagate the pacifist case to a wide audience. The publication of the first issue of *Peace News* on June 6 1936 was the result, financed by donations from members of the study group and their friends. The first issue had a print run of 5000. Humphrey Moore was the only experienced journalist in the group and so it was upon his shoulders that the bulk of the new venture lay. The 'editorial office' was a spare room in his house.

The paper soon came to the attention of Dick Sheppard, the founder of the Peace Pledge Union (PPU), and within a few months *Peace News* became the official organ of the PPU. Despite adverse conditions, the paper's circulation grew impressively. By October 1936 it had reached 6000. A year later this figure had doubled, and by the end of 1938, circulation had steadied at around 20,000 a week — although it did reach a peak of nearly 35,000 in October 1938.

The context of such an impressive circulation during its early years lay in the equally phenomenal growth of the PPU during this period. Its origins dated back to October 1934, when Dick Sheppard published his Peace Letter requesting people to contact him who shared his pacifist commitment, to renounce war and never support or sanction another. The overwhelming response indicated that there existed a strong basis for a pacifist organisation, and in 1936 the PPU was formally constituted. Sheppard based his appeal primarily on the moral repugnance of war and the consequent need for people to take a principled stand against such barbarism. His aim was to create a movement of such magnitude that no government could ignore its influence. As he wrote in 1936, 'If we got, say, a million voters actively insisting that they'll never take part in any war, the Government would have to take notice'.[1]

The popularity of the PPU in those pre-war days, as the *New Statesman* (28.7.36) observed, lay in its appeal 'not only to the convinced absolutist pacifist but to the large number of people with only slight political knowledge but with a recent realisation of the fearful imminence of war, who are fascinated by the direct simplicity of the crusade'. It was the role of *Peace News* to support and service this 'broad church' of a movement, whose members shared little other than their repugnance at the horrors of war. Then, as now, *Peace News*'s columns reflected the range of viewpoints and positions that characterised the peace movement or, rather, peace movements.

Indeed, the aims of peace campaigners can vary enormously, from the absence of organised forms of collective violence between nation states, to compelling visions of 'Heaven on Earth', to the socialist commonwealth, or the anarchist society of small societies founded on co-operation and mutual aid. Different tendencies within the general peace movement have entertained different dreams of peace as an end, so they have also pursued peace by different means. Single-issue campaigners have criticised the 'retreat from reality' of those in co-operative communities who seek peace by leading exemplary nonviolent lifestyles, while 'bourgeois pacifists' have been condemned by those who believe that socialist transformation is a necessary (and perhaps sufficient) condition for peace. Others have focused on industrialism itself, or patriarchy, or the existence of nation states, as the major obstacles to peace. Different tactics and strategies have also been advocated. Supporters of the ballot-box, the pressure group and other pathways of con-stitutional politics have co-existed uneasily with the advocates of direct action, civil disobedience and non-co-operation. Even amongst those who advocate extra-parliamentary methods in pursuit of peace, there have been disagreements over what they mean by nonviolence. Is it just an alternative technique to violence? Or is it a complete philosophy of life?

In other words, the reality of the movement that *Peace News* has sought to serve and inform in its fifty years of continuous publication has been a myriad of different groupings, tendencies, and faiths. The history of *Peace News* is largely a reflection of the

changing balance within the wider movement, and certain
recurring themes can be seen in its pages. Thus, issues that
occupied its columns during the Second World War have to
some extent prefigured debates that have continued to trouble
the peace movement throughout the nuclear age.

Whilst it could be argued that the formal declaration of war
on September 3 1939 meant that the PPU had failed in its basic
purpose, serious questions remained to be faced. The key one
concerned the appropriate role of pacifists in war-time.
Underlying this was the problem of how to reconcile the
promptings of the pacifist conscience with one's duty as a
citizen? Three 'ideal-type' positions were adopted in response
to this dilemma: 'relief', 'resistance' and 'reconstruction'.
Advocating 'relief' were those like Philip Mumford who urged
that pacifists should refrain from opposing government war
measures such as civil defence and conscription, and confine
themselves to humanitarian relief work. They should seek to
soften the blows of war by helping to alleviate the suffering of its
victims. (*Peace News* 1.1.38) The Pacifist Service Corps (later
Bureau) was established by the PPU to assist those pacifists and
conscientious objectors who, in the words of Alex Wood, 'are so
sensitive to the claims of the community on their service, that
they are eager to find some positive and constructive work to do
which is not primarily war work'. (*Peace News* 2.12.40) As
opposed to this strand, the 'resisters' advocated continued
active opposition to war measures. Whilst not objecting to
humanitarian relief work in itself, they urged that the prime
duty of pacifists was to resist war rather than accept it and devote
themselves to ambulance work. It was this element within the
PPU that concentrated on political developments during the
war and used the pages of *Peace News* to campaign for 'Peace by
Negotiation' and, later in the war, tried to launch an 'Armistice
Campaign' against the imposition of a vindictive peace
settlement. By contrast, the third group, the 'reconstructionists',
were those who eschewed engagement in such short-term
protest campaigns, and emphasised the role of pacifists as a
redemptive minority, bearing witness to a higher order of
morality and pointing the way towards a new order of
communal life. Thus, John Middleton Murry, the leading
intellectual force within the PPU during the war years and editor
of *Peace News* from July 1940 to October 1946, likened pacifists
to 'the raw material of a new Christian Church', and sought to

argue that 'socialist communities, prepared for hardship and practised in brotherhood, might be the nucleus of a new Christian society, much as the monasteries were during the dark ages'. (*Peace News* 17.5.40)

It was difficult to object to pacifists engaging in humanitarian relief work which, after all, could be depicted as a principled acknowledgement that we are all responsible for each other. Thus, the main debate and division within the columns of *Peace News* during this period was between the 'resisters' and the 'reconstructionists'. The quietistic focus of the latter group on the role of the pacifist as *witness* and their orientation to a distant vision of an ideal society, rather than campaigning actively on immediate and pressing issues, tested the comprehension of those in the former group, who saw the role of pacifists as that of active *instrument* of peace-making. 'In place of action we have been given moral uplift,' bemoaned Roy Walker at the PPU's AGM in 1941. Bill Grindlay endorsed this criticism, arguing that the repudiation of war did not imply renunciation of the duty to provide answers to immediate problems of concern to the British people, even if this meant that 'in the relative sphere of human politics we have, now as always, to choose the lesser of two evils, and honourably to support the bad against the worse . . .. We cannot philosophise out of the obligations to demand the lesser evil of peace negotiation rather than the greater evil of war'. (*Peace News* 30.5.41)

These different tendencies were all given space in the columns of *Peace News*, although the key editorial figures during the war-period (Middleton Murry and Wilfred Wellock) clearly identified with the reconstructionists — to the extent that in March 1941 they began publishing a monthly supplement under the title of 'Community' to promote the cause of pacifist communities. Yet, despite the differences, the sense of a wider community embracing all shades of pacifist opinion and action emerges clearly from the pages of *Peace News* during the war period. Throughout the war, conscientious objectors and pacifists needed each other for mutual support. They read *Peace News* in part for the assurance that they were not alone in their moral stance, whilst the news of pacifist projects and activities helped reassure them that they had a positive contribution to make to society. Moreover, the difficulties encountered with the printing and distribution of *Peace News* in 1940, after the original printers refused to print the paper and the wholesalers refused to distribute it to the retail outlets, ensured a close relationship between the paper and its readers. (Eric Gill's company printed two issues, each letter set up in type by hand. Then the firm run by Hugh Brock and his brother Ashley took over. Hugh was to remain closely involved with *Peace News* until his death in 1985.) By 1941 somewhere between 18–20,000 copies were being distributed by volunteers up and down the country. It was due to this alternative distribution network that *Peace News* succeeded in making a profit during the war years — for the only time in its life!

The decline in circulation figures to around 9000 a week during the years immediately after the war reflected the decline in the vitality of the peace movement during that period. Pacifists were busy picking up the threads of their interrupted careers and lives. They had less need of each other, and of *Peace News* as an organ of communication and support. Moreover, no longer a persecuted (however mildly) minority, there was not the same need to 'stick together' and the tensions between the different groupings began to reassert themselves. Nowhere were the differences more debilitating than at the centre of the PPU and around *Peace News* itself. At the heart of the problem was Middleton Murry. Although he remained as editor of *Peace News* until 1946, it had become increasingly obvious by the end of the war that he had grown 'increasingly dubious of the position that pacifism is a political method or technique'. (*Peace News* 6.7.45) His loss of faith can be attributed to the revelations of the full extent of the holocaust and his growing anti-communism. When the first reports of the extermination of the Jews began to filter out of Europe in 1943, Murry, along with many pacifists around *Peace News*, tended to dismiss them as allied propaganda. In a provocative review of Arthur Koestler's *The Yogi and the Commissar* in *Peace News* in June 1945, he confessed that he had been a 'mistaken visionary':

> I misjudged two things. First, I misjudged the nature of the average decent man, for whom non-violent resistance is infinitely more difficult and less natural than violent. The second mistake was even more serious. I gravely underestimated the terrible power of scientific terrorism as developed by the totalitarian police-states . . . I am therefore constrained in honesty to admit that under neither the Nazi nor the Soviet system of systematic and applied brutality does non-violent resistance stand a dog's chance . . . In a word, it seems to me that the scientific terrorism of the totalitarian police

state — the wholesale reversion to medieval torture, with all the diabolical ingenuity of applied modern science — has changed the whole frame of reference within which modern pacifism was conceived.

For Murry, the new circumstances required a new form of collective security to ensure world peace, the establishment of a supra-national world authority, equipped with atomic weapons, capable of policing the world arena — a position that was anathema to pacifist readers of *Peace News*. Such was Murry's prestige, however, that he continued to contribute a regular 'Commentary' column after relinquishing the editorship to his protege Frank Lea in 1946. By the time of the 1947 AGM of the PPU, Sybil Morrison was reporting that 95% of PPU groups she had visited had expressed disapproval of Murry's heretical views. In the event, Murry resigned his directorship of *Peace News* in January 1948, having already relinquished his sponsorship of the PPU, maintaining that 'it is now morally impossible for me to remain a Sponsor of a PPU which is definitely opposed to collective security . . .'[2]

Murry, however, had raised fundamental questions which have continued to exercise pacifists since that time: Is nonviolence a feasible stance against totalitarianism and all the forces of repression available to the modern state? How relevant is the individual's refusal to participate in war-making and war-preparation in a nuclear age? If pacifists reject the notion of an 'international police force', have they anything else to offer other than rhetorical affirmations of pacifist ideals?

Certainly, the dismal record of pacifist attempts to construct the cells of a new social commonwealth in the midst of a war-torn world provided little ground for optimism — most of them collapsed once the war ended. To set against this, however, the humanitarian relief work of the Pacifist Service Units continued throughout the war and developed in the post-war period into the Family Service Units, pioneers of intensive family casework in the caring professions. Moreover, as news of starvation conditions in what had been occupied Europe began to emerge, pacifists initiated a Food Relief Campaign and assisted in the formation of 'Save Europe Now', Oxfam and War on Want. A number of pacifists travelled to devastated areas of Europe to help organise and participate in international relief work, especially international work camps: 'pick and shovel peace-making' as *Peace News* described it in February 1950. This was the kind of 'internationalism from below' that began to emerge as the pacifists' response to the collective security arguments of Murry and others. Writing in 1945, Roy Walker had called for an 'assertive pacifism', an 'internationalism from below' that would deprive 'all national governments of the mandate, the power and the means to threaten, prepare or wage war'. (*Peace News* 31.8.45)

The promptings of Roy Walker and others committed to active war resistance encouraged the PPU to establish a Non-violence Commission in 1949 with the task of studying nonviolence as a means of social change and resistance. Their reports on the nonviolent resistance of the Danes and the Norwegians under occupation were of particular interest to the readers of *Peace News*. By the latter half of 1951, this group had begun to plan a number of nonviolent direct action projects of their own against the presence of US air bases in Britain and the manufacture of atomic weapons. Called 'Operation Gandhi', the first action took place outside the War Office on January 1952. It was followed by further actions at Aldermaston, the US airbase at Mildenhall, and at the germ warfare research station at Porton Down.

Although the level of public interest in these actions remained low, the true significance of Operation Gandhi was in the genesis of a movement of nonviolent resistance in *peace-time*, a development in which *Peace News* played a central role. Thus, in 1954 a Pacifist Youth Action Group was formed amongst the voluntary workers at *Peace News*, and it was out of this group of radical pacifists that the Emergency Committee for Direct Action against Nuclear War was formed in April 1957 to act against the British H-bomb tests at Christmas Island. Moreover, in 1960 it was from amongst the members of the Direct Action Committee, with its headquarters at *Peace News*'s offices in Blackstock Road, London, that the activist core of the Committee of 100 emerged. A key figure in the development of this nonviolent action (resistance) wing of the peace movement was Hugh Brock, who had taken over the editorship of *Peace News* from Allen Skinner in 1955. It was under his guidance that *Peace News* developed into a campaigning vehicle for the nuclear disarmament movement following the launch of CND in January 1958. Reports on demonstrations, articles on the danger of radiation, summaries of CND pamphlets, interviews with celebrities of the anti-nuclear movement, alongside serious

Street selling in 1954.

Credit: CNA Photo Service

debates about the morality, legitimacy and political efficacy of nonviolent direct action and civil disobedience, filled the pages of the paper. This concentration on promoting active resistance to the nuclear threat necessarily meant reduced coverage of the issues and campaigns that had attracted *Peace News*'s attention during the first half of the 1950s. During this earlier period *Peace News* had brought to the attention of its readership significant movements for nonviolent social change from around the world, including Vinoba Bhave's land-gift movement in India, Danilo Dolci's work in Sicily, and the emergent civil rights movement in the USA.

The coverage of other liberation movements, especially the colonial freedom movements in Africa and Asia, had presented serious dilemmas for *Peace News*. Just as the issue of the Spanish Civil War had torn apart the No More War Movement in 1936, the problem of the stance to be adopted vis-a-vis movements for change that were prepared to use armed force was a serious one in the 1950s, and has, of course, remained a contentious issue within the peace movement to this day. Writing in 1980, Michael Randle reflected on the period of the 1950s, when *Peace News* tried to present an informed commentary on political events and developments and, at times, supported policies that fell short of the pacifist ideal: 'I know that editors like Allen Skinner were acutely conscious of the tension between what could be said in a commentary on current affairs and the radical nonviolent politics we were working for'. (*Peace News* 30.5.80)

Particular examples of *Peace News*'s support for liberation movements in the Third World during the 1950s include Fenner Brockway's regular column on the anti-colonial struggle, the personal links that were established with Kwame Nkrumah and Kenneth Kaunda, Michael Scott's championing of the people in South West Africa (Namibia), and *Peace News*'s close involvement with the anti-apartheid struggle which led to the banning of the paper in South Africa in 1959. This sympathy with liberation movements prepared to countenance armed struggle, the active support of unconstitutional measures of direct action, and the focus on a campaign against one aspect of modern war (nuclear weapons) rather than against the institution of war itself, caused concern to many of the more absolutist pacifists of the PPU. In a typically provocative piece in *Peace News* (8.8.58) called 'The map of Mrs Brown', Reginald Reynolds delineated some of the divisions within the pacifist movement in the late

1950s. There was the pacifist 'old guard':

> They are good old sloggers who cling bravely to the belief that the
> slogans and activities which have been proved and tested by
> decades of dismal failure deserve our allegiance and will at any
> moment lead on to victory.

Then there were the 'perfectionists' who,

> having proved that there can be no peace without a complete social,
> political, economic, psychological and spiritual revolution, they
> nevertheless leave me with an awkward feeling that they are talking
> very good sense about town planning when the immediate and
> urgent necessity is for a fire engine, which they reject as a
> palliative.

The third group were the 'firefighters' who were driven by a
desperate sense of urgency and a passion for action, but for
Reynolds they appeared to lack 'any real understanding of what
they are up against'.

It was clear that *Peace News* had come under the sway of the
'firefighters', and the concentration on the 'resistance' mode of
peace-making caused some dismay amongst the other groupings.
Wilfred Wellock, the most prominent advocate of the 'reconstruction' mode, complained about 'the dearth of materials
on the social revolution that ought to be appearing regularly in
Peace News' and bemoaned the fact that Hugh Brock had
become 'so overwhelmed with the nuclear weapon campaign'.[3]

Sybil Morrison, the Chairperson of the PPU, was particularly
upset by *Peace News*'s wholehearted support of the nuclear
disarmament campaign. She was unable to accept Hugh
Brock's argument that nuclear disarmament would be a
significant 'first step' towards total disarmament:

> . . . it is my conviction that nuclear weapons do, and probably will
> continue to, deter nuclear war. Their abandonment has no
> appearance to me of a 'first step' . . . on the contrary, . . . I even
> think governments might decide to abandon it, and far from being
> one step nearer may be even more than ever convinced of the
> necessity of other quite appalling weapons . . . I think it is the kind
> of half measure which may prevent and will certainly deter, if it
> were successful, the coming of total disarmament perhaps for ever.
> I cannot water down my pacifism in order to support an
> organisation with whose aims I disagree.[4]

The strength of feeling was such that the decision was taken to sever the formal ties between the PPU and *Peace News* in the spring of 1961. Hugh Brock attempted to reassure those who feared that an independent *Peace News* might weaken its commitment to 'the sheet anchor of 100 per cent pacifism': 'We shall not cast [it] away. What we *don't* want to do is to use that sheet anchor to keep the vessel in harbour. We hope it will be stowed safely on board as we sail out into the troubled waters where we have a job of rescue work to do for the war-threatened people of the world.'[5]

Free from the need to look over its shoulder, the paper was now at liberty to explore the implications of radical pacifism in the nuclear age. A central feature of the analysis that began to emerge was drawn from the experience of direct action against the nuclear threat — people *acting*, refusing to be passive, seeking to participate in the determination of their future. From this there developed a concern to foster a reversal of the flow of power, a democratisation of all areas of institutional life — the advocacy of workers' control in the economic sphere, and regional devolution and decentralisation in the realm of politics. *Peace News* also revived the idea of a Third Force which it had advocated in the mid-1950s, the notion of a positive alignment of independent voices and nations as a creative force for peace, a Third Way transcending the polar divisions between the super-powers in the international arena and moving beyond the party-political divisions in the domestic sphere. (This idea of a Third Force was taken up in the 1980s by the theorists of the European Nuclear Disarmament (END) movement. Thus, E P Thompson has referred to a 'third way' beyond the hegemony of the super-powers, and has called for a 'detente of peoples rather than states'. See E P Thompson, *Beyond the Cold War*, London: Merlin, 1982, p 29.)

In exploring this wider vision of peace, *Peace News* was very much part of the intellectual ferment of the New Left that followed the crushing of the Hungarian Revolution in 1956. This trend was further strengthened by the appointment of Theodor Roszak as editor on the retirement of Hugh Brock in 1964. By this time the heat had begun to go out of the direct action and the constitutional wings of the nuclear disarmament movement. Drawing on the United States experience of Students for a Democratic Society, Roszak argued that the 'war issue' was too remote from the daily concerns of the mass of people, hence the 'failure' to generate a movement of sufficient

Hugh Brock (left), editor from 1955-64, interviewing Commander Albert Bigelow on his way back to the USA from the Delhi-Peking Friendship March organised by the World Peace Brigade in 1963.

numbers to achieve nuclear disarmament. A wider definition of violence was required, social as well as nuclear, that embraced racial inequality, poor housing conditions, and poverty in all its many dimensions. Pacifists should apply their methods of direct action to such issues which were of immediate concern to people in their everyday lives. In urging a widening of the radical pacifist perspective, Roszak was also reinforcing a trend that had already developed amongst some Briish radical pacifists, who had begun to argue that if nuclear disarmament was to be achieved, the apathy and sense of powerlessness experienced by the mass of people had to be overcome. It was argued that if one worked on 'small issues' like housing conditions and the like, the resulting sense of empowerment, of having some control over one's life, could and would feed into the campaign over 'big issues' like nuclear disarmament. Thus, in an editorial 'Letter to an Easter Marcher' in April 1965, *Peace News* expressed its reservations about the narrow focus of CND, observing that

> a campaign which talks about the dignity of human life must, if it takes itself seriously, concern itself with day-to-day problems and injustices as well as with the all-embracing problem of war. *Peace News* is dedicated to building up this non-violent movement of ideas and action.

In pursuance of this end *Peace News*, by the mid-1960s, was devoting an increased proportion of space to 'social issues' such as education, psychiatry, housing, race relations, new technology, prisons and the treatment of offenders, poverty and so on. As part of this process of widening the area of concern, an increase in the coverage of new developments in the arts also took place. At the same time *Peace News* remained true to its role as an agency of active war resistance. From the early 1960s Adam Roberts had begun to write about the struggle in Vietnam, well before it became an international issue that mobilised concerned people around the world. *Peace News* continued to focus on the potential role of the Buddhists as a creative 'Third Force' opposed to the US-backed regime in the South, but independent from the Soviet-supported national forces. *Peace News* also continued its support of the Greek peace movement and imprisoned prisoners of conscience in Greece and elsewhere in the world. By the middle of 1968, the Nigerian Civil War and the plight of the Biafrans began to dominate the paper, whilst the emergence of the civil rights movement in Northern Ireland was also demanding attention.

It was during this period of the late 1960s that *Peace News* began to move towards a synthesis of the three modes of peace action and thought that characterised the peace movement during the Second World War. The focus on community action for social change combined a humanitarian concern to relieve suffering, a campaigning style that drew upon the direct action tradition of the war resistance movement, and a vision of a decentralised and radically democratised social order. This latter was a direct continuation of the libertarian tradition of ethical socialism that had been a crucial component of pacifist communitarian thinking in the 1940s. In a more obvious link with the earlier 'reconstructionists', *Peace News* also began to advocate the creation of 'counter-institutions' and alternative structures as a form of positive action that went beyond 'banning the bomb'. 'Peace is beautiful, live it' announced an editorial in May 1967.

These developments took place in the context of a serious quest to develop a 'pacifism for peace-time'. The aim was to be both relevant and practical, by addressing issues of immediate concern to people, and 'utopian' in the sense of not losing sight of the pacifist vision of a nonviolent world. In a series of editorials that appeared early in 1968, entitled 'Towards a definition of ourselves', *Peace News* tried to spell out its developing position, one best depicted as anarcho-pacifism: a fusion of the anarchist critique of the state and the pacifist critique of violence as a means of revolutionary transformation. The term 'nonviolent revolution' began to appear, referring to a liberatory 'movement of movements', the task of *Peace News* being to act as a link between the different movements, seeking to join radicals in different areas into a new resistance movement opposed to war and war-preparation, but also exploring ways of constructing a mass nonviolent movement for a new society. Defining itself as one of the building blocks of this new society, *Peace News* began to transform its own internal organisation. The post of editor had been dispensed with in 1967 and an editorial collective formed. In 1970 a serious attempt to break down the traditional division between the writers and readers of the paper began with the introduction of regular meetings between staff and supporters. This trend was taken further in 1971 when a new 'Peace News Company' was formed to involve more people in the responsibility of running the paper. It was at this time, also, that the sub-title 'For Nonviolent Revolution' began to appear on the front page of the paper.

The context for this re-evaluation of the paper — the late 1960s and early 1970s — was a heady time, when the campaign against the Vietnam War was at its height, student radicalism was in the ascendant, and a whole range of traditional assumptions, values and patterns of life were being brought into question by the proponents of an 'alternative society'. The staff at *Peace News* were caught up in this general political and cultural movement. Discussions of the role of drugs in the process of cultural transformation began to appear in the paper, four-letter words began to creep into articles — there was even a graphic of a 'copulating couple' on the front page of August 11, 1972. Traditional readers of the paper remained unconvinced that the theme of 'Make love, not war' needed to be illustrated quite so explicitly.

And yet, at a time when the general trend of the paper was towards the 'reconstruction' mode of peace-making and a questioning of the fundamental assumptions underpinning the key institutions of society, the active war-resisting tradition was not forsaken. *Peace News*'s coverage of the Biafran tragedy widened to a humanitarian concern with relieving the famine situation that had accompanied the civil war, whilst its coverage and analysis of the struggle for civil rights by the Catholic minority in Northern Ireland had deepened. Throughout 1969 *Peace News* carried regular reports on the nonviolent demonstrations by which the civil rights movement brought pressure on the Unionist power structure. In 1970, after the British Army had been sent in, Bob Overy, a co-editor of *Peace News*, went to live in a Protestant working class district of Belfast. He began to contribute a series of thoughtful and perceptive articles on the conflict and the problems associated with developing an appropriate pacifist response — one which rejected the use of the army as a stabilising force and the use of British pow~ 'modernise' the society, and which looked to the dev~' of a genuine non-sectarian alliance between commu~ in the working class communities as the basis for solution. Another of *Peace News*'s co-editors, Roger ~ instrumental in developing initiatives over Nami~ launching 'Operation Omega' — an attempt to get ~

Bengal following its invasion by West Pakistan in 1971. *Peace News* also published a number of issues of 'Rainbow' as a supplement — a newsletter serving the network of Nonviolent Action Groups that had developed in the wake of trips to Britain by two North American nonviolent activists, George Lakey and Lynne Shivers.

Despite the significance of these attempts to mobilise opinion and action against the continuing horrors of war and collective violence, the main trend of the paper during the early 1970s was towards a whole-hearted identification with the emergent alternative society and the various attempts to construct the seeds of a new social order at the interstices of the old. As John Papworth wrote in one of his regular columns in January 1973: 'Our concern is peace. And the nature of the kind of social order that will produce peace as naturally as our present ones produce war is surely, in the difficult and no doubt confusing times ahead, our first priority'. Thus, by the mid-1970s the dominant focus of the paper was on such themes as women's liberation and sexual politics, communes and co-operatives, free schools, alternative economics and technology. The stress was upon the individual's responsibility to examine every aspect of their life and to restructure it in the direction of liberation and the non-exploitation of others and the environment.

The editorial collective began to examine aspects of their own lives, and argued that the integrity of the paper demanded that its structural base be consistent with its social analysis, which emphasised the creation of new nonviolent modes of organising individual and collective life. They proposed that *Peace News* should move out of London to the provinces and organise itself as a printing and publishing co-operative producing a fortnightly paper. The change in format, frequency and location of *Peace News* was also intended to enable the staff to become more closely involved in the various grass-roots initiatives that were springing up, and thereby improve the quality of the reporting and analysis of this 'reconstructionist' movement. This proposal was met with considerable opposition by those in and around *Peace News* who remained firmly committed to the 'resistance' mode of peace-making and peace action. It was alleged that in moving away from London and in coming out only once every two weeks, *Peace News* would be abrogating its traditional role as campaigning agency for the peace movement, keeping ists informed of the latest news and developments relevant to the struggle for peace. (It was proposed that a London-based paper with a campaigning emphasis should be published to complement the new *Peace News*, but this came to nothing.) After a somewhat acrimonious debate, the decision was finally taken to move to Nottingham, where *Peace News* had been offered free premises, and on June 21, 1974 the first issue from the new base was published —with the editorial collective affirming: 'We want to relate personal experience and living to politics; we are making our style of working reflect our philosophy more closely'. As part of this self-conscious identification with the growing counter-cultural movement for an alternative society, *Peace News* began to publish the CLAP catalogue. This 'Community Levy for Alternative Projects' was an experiment in alternative economics — a kind of mail-order catalogue of alternative projects which people were invited to support with donations by means of a 'community levy' on their incomes.

Perhaps somewhat paradoxically, at a time when *Peace News* consciously moved from being a weekly *newspaper* in order to develop a more 'in-depth' treatment of the many trends and themes of the heterogeneous movement for an alternative society, the paper won a national 'Scoop of the Year' award for its revelations about plans to establish a strike-breaking 'private army', 'Great Britain 1975'. Moreover, the paper continued with its campaigning war resisting tradition through its active involvement with the British Withdrawal from Northern Ireland Campaign (BWNIC). *Peace News* had been central to the launching of BWNIC in 1973 and had continued to be the main organ of the campaign, especially during 1975, when 14 supporters (including a member of the *Peace News* collective and a couple of ex-members) were charged, though later acquitted, under the Incitement to Disaffection Act. Two years later the collective and the *Peace News* Company itself were charged with contempt of court after the publication of the name of a prosecution witness in an Official Secrets case brought against two journalists and a former soldier. It took a successful appeal at the House of Lords to remove the threat of bankruptcy facing the paper. This defiance of the state through the publication of 'official secrets' was reminiscent of the heady days of the early 1960s, when *Peace News*, as the chief organ of the direct action wing of the nuclear disarmament movement, had supported the 'Spies for Peace' in 1963, following their uncovering of the state's plans for ruling Britain in the event of a nuclear war or similar emergency. (Amongst other noteworthy 'scoops' of *Peace News*, were the revelations concerning British atrocities in Kenya in 1956, whilst in the late 1960s, *Peace News*'s coverage of the Biafran tragedy brought to the public much information which failed to reach the columns of the mass media.)

Despite the paper's concern with developing a close involvement with the grass-roots initiatives of the embryonic alternative society during the mid-1970s, it continued to give prominent coverage to a range of nonviolent movements of resistance around the world. These included the anti-militarist struggle at Larzac in France, the campaign of the farm workers for union recognition in California, the Women's Liberation Movement, the struggle of minority groups and indigenous peoples around the globe, the development of the ecology movement in general, and the initiatives of Greenpeace in particular in opposing French nuclear testing in the Pacific.

In the latter half of the 1970s, particular prominence was given to the emergence of the campaigns against nuclear power that had developed at Wyhl in West Germany, Malville in France, and Seabrook in the USA. The organisational pattern of affinity groups developed by the Clamshell Alliance at Seabrook was of particular interest to *Peace News*, and when it was proposed to construct a nuclear power plant at Torness in Scotland, *Peace News* was influential in shaping the nature of the campaign along the lines of autonomous affinity groups and alliances that had been developed at Seabrook, and performed a crucial role as a communication agency and discussion forum for the different local groups. Indeed, it was during this period of the late 1970s that *Peace News* established the kind of organic linkage with the new resistance movement against nuclear power that had characterised its relationship with the nuclear disarmament movement of the late 1950s and early 1960s. However, the nature of the paper and of the movement had changed over the years. Just as *Peace News* had organised itself into a collective and had sought to embody the principles of the alternative nonviolent society in its working practices and its relationship with its readers,[6] so the new movement was seeking to develop through the organisational form of affinity groups a model of how a nonviolent, non-exploitative social order might be co-ordinated with an emphasis on decentralised power and participatory, non-hierarchical methods of decision-making.

Although, to some extent, *Peace News* was caught unawares by the rapid revival of the nuclear disarmament movement in the 1980s, the new form of that movement owed something to the analysis and organisational forms developed by the anti-nuclear power movement. *Peace News* has played a role in the development of a number of features of this contemporary peace movement: the emphasis on non-hierarchical, participatory ways of organising for direction action, the increased awareness of the relationship between nuclear weapons and nuclear power, and the growing recognition of the linkages between the many forms of domination that permeate the nuclear state and civil society. Perhaps one of the clearest statements of *Peace News*'s position with regard to the nuclear disarmament issue appeared in an editorial of October 16 1981:

It probably won't surprise you that *Peace News* is committed to unilateral nuclear disarmament and the dismantling of nuclear weapons worldwide. It may be less obvious to you why the paper covers a wide range of other issues, from sexual politics to Third World struggles. They are not just a random assortment of issues that should concern radical lefties; in our analysis they are all intimately linked, and we should be fooling ourselves to strive for a change in one area, say, to achieve "peace", while others remain unchanged.

The nuclear arms race is not just the work of a few evil or misguided people at the top, but has its roots in the structure and attitudes of centralised, industrial society, where relationships are power relationships: government over "ordinary" people, rich nations over poor, men over women. The threat of war will stay with us as long as these patterns of dominance and submission exist. So we must not just press for nuclear disarmament, but work to change the structure of society and the relationships between the people and countries.

Opposition to the arms race, racism, sexism, injustice, and the centralised state must be coupled with the creation of positive alternatives. This means initiating and supporting moves for decentralisation and autonomy, such as local energy groups, shared child-care and education, self-help health groups, and workers' co-operatives. It means taking responsibility for our own lives, fighting our own sexism and racism, and our own dependence on the state.

Nonviolent revolution entails taking back the power that has been taken from us, and refusing to exercise illegitimate power over anyone else, whether that power be domestic tyranny, economic exploitation or the threat of military force. (emphasis added)

This emphasis on the need to combine active struggle against domination, oppression and exploitation in all areas of life with the more positive task of creating alternatives to the nonviolent structures of society has continued to characterise *Peace News*'s approach to the nuclear threat, which remains the major concern of the wider peace movement. As such, it marks a significant step towards the synthesis of the two main traditions of peace-making that have been the hallmark of *Peace News* over the last 50 years — resistance and reconstruction, two sides of the same movement for a nonviolent society.

1. A Huxley and H R L Sheppard, *100,000 Say No*, London: PPU, 1936, p 6.
2. Letter to S Morris, *PPU Journal*, August 16, 1947.
3. Letters to Ernest Bader, April 15 & 27, 1959.
4. Sybil Morrison to Hugh Brock, April 9 and April 14, 1958. (Hugh Brock archives, Commonweal Collection)
5. Letter from Hugh Brock to 'friends', May 4, 1961. (Hugh Brock archives)
6. PN made repeated attempts to encourage readers to feel that it was *their* paper. In 1969 a series of Potlatches (weekend meetings on specific topics of interest to PN readers) had been initiated. These were replaced by Readers' Meetings that took place several times a year and which made recommendations to the staff of the paper.

Author's note: I am particularly grateful to Bob Overy for his criticisms and comments on an earlier draft of this chapter.

Pacifism, War Resistance, and the Struggle Against Nuclear Weapons

Part I: From Conscientious Objection to Nonviolent Resistance

by Michael Randle

Emrys Hughes, in a foreword to Hugh Brock's *Peace News* pamphlet, 'The Century of Total War', noted the difference between the situation of conscientious objectors and those who made a deliberate decision to take part in nonviolent obstruction at military bases in the early 1960s. He wrote, recalling his experience as a conscientious objector during World War I:

> Mine was not a voluntary sit-down strike outside a military camp, it was a compulsory one. I had to choose between going into the Army and going to jail, so I chose jail and never regretted the choice. But the choice of the young opponent of war today is rather different. This young generation has wisely decided to make their stand before the war begins, for if war comes now, there will not be a time or opportunity to make any effective form of personal protest — we will all be victims of the H-Bomb.

My purpose in this contribution is briefly to trace this shift from the notion of *conscientious objection* to that of *conscientious resistance* since the Second World War, and to note the role that *Peace News* played in this development.

The notion of organising a general strike against war had had a considerable following among socialists before World War I. In the event it came to nothing, and war resistance chiefly took the form of a conscientious refusal to participate in the holocaust by tens of thousands of young people in Britain and other countries. The anti-war organisation of the 1920s and 1930s grew directly from that resistance. Thus the No More War movement was the successor to the wartime No-Conscription Fellowship, and it in turn merged with the newly formed Peace

Pledge Union in the 1930s. War Resisters International, the organisation linking anti-war movements in different countries, was founded in 1921 with Fenner Brockway, himself a wartime objector, its first chairman.

It was Gandhi's campaigns of mass nonviolent resistance to British imperial rule that were chiefly responsible for a resurgence of interest during the 1930s in using direct action to resist war preparations in peacetime, and to bring war to a rapid halt if it should occur. Here the classic text is the Appendix to Bart de Ligt's *The Conquest of Violence*, published in an English translation in 1937. Even today, almost half a century after its publication, it is striking for its imaginative radicalism. De Ligt's book and Appendix, together with Aldous Huxley's *Ends and Means*, Richard Gregg's *The Conquest of Violence* and some of the writings of the American pacifist A J Muste, were to influence the thinking of the group round *Peace News*, intent on initiating anti-war, and especially anti-nuclear, protest in the early period after the Second World War.

Peace News itself set the process in motion in the early war years, publishing, in October 1941, a series of three articles by Roy Walker on nonviolent resistance. Walker subsequently drew up the terms of reference of a Non-Violence Commission set up in 1949 by the Peace Pledge Union (of which *Peace News* was at that time still the official journal). The terms of reference enjoined the group, among other things, to study 'appropriate types of self-discipline and public demonstration', the pattern of a nonviolent economy for Britain and 'the aims and methods of a nonviolent foreign policy for Britain, with some indication of suitable individual or small group demonstrations practicable in present conditions'.

By 1951, some of the members of that Commission felt it was time to move from discussion to action. An example had been set during that year by the nonviolent blockade of an army camp in Wales by seventy Welsh Nationalists, including Gwynfor Evans, President of Plaid Cymru, to protest against the seizure of the land by the War Office. In December 1951, several members of the Non-Violence Commission formed a new group, Operation Gandhi, to organise nonviolent direct action. Their political goals were the withdrawal of US troops from Britain, ending the manufacture by Britain of atomic weapons, British withdrawal from NATO and the disbanding of the British Armed Forces. In January 1952, fourteen members of

Operation Gandhi, seven women and seven men, staged a sit-down outside the War Office in Whitehall and were arrested and fined. Two of those taking part, Hugh Brock and Harry Mister, were staff members of *Peace News*; several others were closely associated with the paper. The War Office sitdown received some publicity in the national press, including the *Daily Mail*, which published a photograph with a news item underneath which began 'This is no place to squat' but it was *Peace News* that gave it major coverage and published the statement put out by the group. The paper also continued to report the pioneering demonstrations of the early and mid-fifties as it was to do with the larger scale demonstrations later on.

The secretary of Operation Gandhi was Hugh Brock, one of the Second World War generation of conscientious objectors who had joined *Peace News* as an Assistant Editor in 1946. He was to play a leading role in the development of anti-nuclear direct action in this country. His combination of personal self-effacement and good humour on the one hand, and energy, perseverence and organising ability on the other were exactly the qualities the movement needed, given its intention to challenge the public and the authorities through radical action, while continuing to engage them in rational dialogue.

My own association with Operation Gandhi began shortly after the Whitehall sit-down of 1952, which I read about in the first copy of *Peace News* I ever bought after I had registered as a conscientious objector to conscription. It brought me into contact with a number of impressive people besides Hugh Brock himself. I remember especially Kathleen Rawlins, a Quaker woman who had reflected deeply on the implications for public action of the Gandhian nonviolent tradition. She wrote, or at least played a major part in writing, the leaflets produced by the group and did much to establish the particular style of nonviolent protest in that period. Hugh Brock, for example, in his pamphlet mentioned earlier, recalls that it was on her insistence that the group informed the police in advance of their intention to sit down in front of the War Office, and this tradition of openness was maintained right through the period of the Direct Action Committee and for at least the first year of the Committee of 100's existence in the early sixties. Another interesting member was Tom Wardle, a clergyman who had known Gandhi and had taken part in passive resistance in South Africa. He also joined the staff of *Peace News* in the mid-fifties and his main interest was in the idea of building a 'Congress of England' to create a decentralised, self-reliant society in this country. (Like most members of the group, he also supported the notion of independence for Wales and Scotland, which he hoped would establish Congresses of their own.)

Support during the early 1950s for Operation Gandhi — which was soon to change its name to the Non-Violent Resistance Group — remained on a small scale and its public impact was minimal. Its importance lay in the pioneering demonstrations it undertook, the national and international network of nonviolent activists it established, and the internal political debate it stimulated on the use of direct action in a parliamentary democracy. (Curiously, however, the debate on this issue did not figure in *Peace News* itself until the late 1950s, following the larger and better-publicised demonstrations of the Direct Action Committee.)

During the early 1950s, Operation Gandhi/Non-Violent Resistance Group organised demonstrations, usually of around thirty or forty people: at the USAF base at Mildenhall in Suffolk (July 1952) where two women, Dorothy Morton and Connie Jones, lay on the road in front of the main entrance; at Aldermaston (April 1952), then still under construction and styling itself 'The Atomic Energy Research Establishment'; at the Microbiological Research Establishment at Porton Down (March 1953); at AERE Harwell (April 1953), and again at Aldermaston in September 1953.

Discussions with visiting nonviolent activists chiefly from the United States and India, were an important feature of the Non-Violent Resistance Group meetings. Bayard Rustin, the American civil rights activist who later co-ordinated the 1963 March on Washington was one who spoke to the group. Bill Sutherland, also a Black American, was another. Both were to play an important part in later nonviolent actions. Bayard made a keynote speech in Trafalgar Square at Easter 1958, at the beginning of the Aldermaston March; he has also stated that it was the success of the Aldermaston march that gave him the idea of proposing the mass march on Washington. Bill Sutherland was a key contact in Ghana, where he had gone to live, when the Direct Action Committee in Britain and the Committee for Non-Violent Action in the US initiated the international Sahara Protest Expedition which set out from Accra in December 1959 to try to reach the French A-Bomb test site in the Sahara. The close links with *Peace News*, especially through the person of Hugh Brock, were important in extending the international outreach of the Non-Violent Resistance Group.

Hugh became editor of the paper in 1955 and remained so until 1964. His involvement from the earliest days in anti-nuclear weapons campaigning accounts in part for the major and thoughtful coverage this was given in the paper during the crucial years when it developed into a mass movement. He also built up a staff of writer-activists committed to developing Gandhian nonviolent action in the anti-militarist cause, including, at various periods, such key people as April Carter (secretary of the Direct Action Committee from 1958 to 1961), Alan Lovell (also on the DAC and a founder member of the *Universities and Left Review*), and Adam Roberts and Gene Sharp (both to become academic specialists in the study of nonviolent resistance).

The shift from the early pioneering efforts to effective public protest dates from around 1957. It was in that year that Harold and Sheila Steele and others volunteered to attempt to sail into the British H-Bomb Testing Area at Christmas Island in the Pacific. The emergency organising committee to raise funds for, and co-ordinate, the project was again a *Peace News* grouping. Allen Skinner, who edited the paper in the early to mid 1950s, acted as its secretary, closely supported by Hugh Brock.

Harold Steele got no further than Japan, but the project aroused a great deal of public interest and support and coincided with a new mood in Britain, following the Suez aggression of the previous year and the Soviet invasion of Hungary. In November 1957, supporters of the Christmas Island project met in London, established the Direct Action Committee Against Nuclear War on a firm basis, and agreed to hold a three-day march from London to Aldermaston the following Easter.

There is not space to recount here the history of the public protests and direct action organised from 1958 onwards by the Direct Action Committee, the Committee of 100 and the Campaign for Nuclear Disarmament. However, I do want to stress the continuity, in terms of ideas, experience and people between the small scale endeavours of the early 1950s and the later successful public actions; I also want to stress the role of *Peace News* as a centre of organisation and as a forum for the development of ideas on nonviolent action.

The proposal for a three-day march to Aldermaston was made by Laurence Brown and Hugh Brock as a direct result of their experience in organising protests there in 1952 and 1953. Pat Arrowsmith was employed as secretary to organise the march and was installed in an office at *Peace News*, then located in Finsbury Park, North London. A March Committee comprising Hugh Brock, Pat Arrowsmith, the Labour MP Frank Allaun, Walter Wolfgang and me, was set up and met regularly to discuss tactics and organisational questions. Sometime fairly late in the preparations, Michael Howard was asked to take charge of marshalling the demonstration and did a first-class job, recruiting and briefing people for this work. A briefing leaflet enjoining a strict nonviolent discipline was also prepared and distributed to all march participants. This was mainly drafted by Gene Sharp, who had joined the staff of *Peace News* in the mid-1950s and had made a special study of Gandhi's campaigning methods. My memory of the period leading up to the march is of experiencing alternating feelings of exhilaration and panic. Exhilaration because support for the march grew beyond our wildest imaginings; panic because, as the *Peace News* lines became jammed with telephone calls, it seemed impossible to imagine how our tiny group could cope with the organisational problems that this degree of support had thrown up.

It was during this hectic period that the DAC adopted the now famous nuclear disarmament symbol when Gerald Holtom, an artist from Twickenham, came to see Hugh Brock, Pat Arrowsmith and me, one night at the *Peace News* office and showed us his design. Shortly afterwards, when our first leaflets appeared bearing the symbol, I recall a veteran of earlier campaigns complaining to me that we must have been out of our minds when we adopted it; it had no meaning, he said, and it would never catch on.

After the success of the Aldermaston March, the Direct Action Committee went on to organise other highly publicised demonstrations, notably the occupations and sit-downs at the Thor rocket base at North Pickenham in December 1958 which resulted in the first arrests and prison sentences; industrial campaigns in 1959 and 1960 in which Pat Arrowsmith was particularly active; the Sahara Protest Expedition of 1959–60, which had a very considerable impact in Africa and was followed by a Pan-African conference in Accra in April 1960 to co-ordinate efforts against colonialism and 'nuclear imperialism'; the European end of the San Francisco-Moscow March in 1960–61, which was co-ordinated by April Carter (appointed secretary of the DAC in 1958 when Pat Arrowsmith became Field Secretary); and finally the Polaris demonstrations at Holy Loch at Whitsun 1961. *Peace News* coverage of, and debates around, these actions, and subsequently of the Committee of 100 actions, were unmatched anywhere else in the press in Britain, even after the demonstrations were making front-page headlines.

Meanwhile the Campaign for Nuclear Disarmament had been formed in 1958 and, thanks in part to the Aldermaston March, had developed rapidly into a mass popular movement which organised Aldermaston marches on an ever larger scale in the subsequent five years. October 1960 saw the formation of the Committee of 100, which organised a series of mass sit-down demonstrations in Central London during the first nine months of 1961, beginning with a demonstration of approximately 5,000 people outside the Ministry of Defence in February and culminating in the sit-down of somewhere between 12,000 and 17,000 people in Trafalgar Square in September. The latter was also co-ordinated with the largest direct action demonstration up to that time at a military base, when 500 people took part in a blockade at Holy Loch organised by the recently formed Scottish Committee of 100. Although the size of demonstrations declined after the high point of September 1961, the Committee of 100 remained in existence until 1968, gave rise to parallel organisations and inspired similar campaigning methods in other countries, notably in Greece, and popularised the whole notion of taking nonviolent direct action, not only in relation to the nuclear issue but in relation to other social and political questions. If CND today can organise sit-down demonstrations at military bases without causing a major split in the movement, or even arousing any particularly sharp controversy, this is due in large measure to the fact that the DAC and Committee of 100, in close collaboration with *Peace News*, succeeded in establishing nonviolent direct action as a recognised part of the political culture.

But was the shift from conscientious objection to nonviolent obstruction, and from purely constitutional protest to acts of

The Polaris Action Group, organised by the Direct Action Committee, attempted to obstruct US Polaris submarines on the Holy Loch in May 1961. A sub and the US supply ship are visible in the background.

civil disobedience justified in a parliamentary democracy? This was one of the crucial debates of the period, and one where the direct actionists had to acquit themselves well if their methods were to be more widely adopted. Here again *Peace News*, far more than any other paper or journal to the centre and left of British politics, provided a forum for the debate — as it did for all the discussions about the ethics, strategy and tactics of anti-nuclear campaigning in the DAC and Committee of 100 years. In December 1958 and January 1959, in the aftermath of the DAC's North Pickenham demonstrations, the paper carried a series of articles discussing this issue, starting with a debate between Allen Skinner and me in the issue of 19 December 1958 and closing with a long contribution from Gene Sharp in the issue of 30 January 1959.

Re-reading the debate, I am particularly struck by the quality and tone of many of the contributions, especially of those by Allen Skinner and Damaris Parker Rhodes, who put the case against nonviolent obstruction in the British situation. Allen Skinner argued that, in a democracy, the minority had to be sensitive to the views of the majority, as well as the other way round, and that the North Pickenham demonstration involved a form of coercion which could not be justified in the British context and would not be effective; there could be, he argued, 'no coercive short cut'. (Allen Skinner, it should be noted, was a member of the Direct Action Committee and was himself to spend two months in prison in 1960 when all the members of the committee then in the country were arrested. As a conscientious objector during the First World War he had contracted surgical TB as a result of the appalling prison conditions endured during two successive prison sentences of 253 days and 141 days respectively). Damaris Parker Rhodes (PN 2 Jan 1959) was not opposed to the same degree as Allen Skinner. In some circumstances, she argued, nonviolent obstruction would be morally justified, but in this instance the constitutional avenues had not yet been fully explored.

The most crucial point made by the advocates of direct action was, I think, that democracy depended not only on the concept of majority rule, but on respect for basic human rights. Where a government policy, however much public support it could command, denied the basic rights either of its own citizens or of people in other countries, there was a democratic duty to oppose it, and, if necessary, obstruct its implementation by nonviolent action. Preparations for nuclear war constituted, at least potentially, the most horrendous denial of human rights in history, and if nuclear war was to be resisted it had to be before the event.

Underlying the contributions of those supporting direct action, and referred to specifically by Gene Sharp in his article, was the sense of a world in crisis and the need to act before it was too late. For many of the participants in the direct action demonstrations, this sense of peril was, I think, an important motivating factor. (And, as the Cuban missile crisis in 1962 was to demonstrate, it was well founded.) Gene Sharp in his contribution also made an important point about the potential effectiveness of nonviolent direct action, arguing that the social reality of war preparations had to be met not simply with words, but with an alternative social reality that could be dramatised and made concrete by the nonviolent action.

The debate remains relevant at the present time. Indeed I am concerned that today direct action may sometimes be undertaken too casually, without sufficient thought being given as to when and in what forms it is justified, and how it might mesh with more conventional forms of political action to bring about the desired goals. Given the resurgence of nonviolent action against nuclear war preparations in the 1980s, *Peace News* might perform a valuable service today by reviving and extending the earlier debate.

Part 11: 1962 to the Present
by Diana Shelley

What led to the decline of the nuclear disarmament movement after 1962? There is no simple answer. My own reason for leaving at the time was that I could not bear the quarrelling within the Committee of 100. But there had been deep divisions within the different organisations even at the height of the movement which, perhaps, merely became more painful as the numbers decreased. The principal organisations of the peace movement were even more deeply antagonistic, though individuals worked across the divisions. The Peace Pledge

Union still refused to campaign on the 'limited' issue of nuclear weapons; CND shunned the more radical activists of the Committee of 100 and denounced the anarchists; the Committee of 100 adopted ever more radical positions and diverse issues.

What had united the movement initially was the simple aim to 'ban the bomb'. The emphasis was on action rather than analysis; the strategies for that action were very different. The Committee of 100's strategy of civil disobedience aimed to immobilise the government by filling the jails, but even if it could have been made to work, this was never a viable strategy by itself. All too often it degenerated into the tactic of the sit-down, where decreasing numbers mattered too much.

CND, on the other hand, relied on 'conventional' campaigning, pressure group politics, and the hope of influencing the Labour Party. Its leadership had never been very accountable and began to appear even less so; its policy document *Steps Towards Peace* (November 1962), an attempt at a political strategy, was widely seen as a betrayal of the simple 'moral' campaign for unilateral nuclear disarmament. Both organisations were accused of having been 'infiltrated' — CND by the Communists, the Committee of 100 by anarchists.

Both tended to rely on the 'novelty' of their demonstrations (the 'dignified' mass march or the, equally dignified, sit-down) without seeing those methods of demonstrating as techniques in a broader political campaign which needed to be developed on all levels if it were to attract and sustain a mass movement.

None of these factors were responsible in themselves for the decline. The Cuban missile crisis of October 1962 struck deeply at many people's faith in their own power. Even Adam Roberts, then *Peace News*' news editor, wrote that 'there is very little that peace movements can do to affect the course of such a crisis . . . [It] had the effect of paralysing and immobilising people. Many felt that if things were out of control it was no use pretending otherwise, and stayed at home . . . .' Some of them stayed there for a long time.

Ironically, the Partial Test Ban Treaty of the following year may have had the same effect: we had accomplished something and the very fact of an agreement between the super-powers boded well, so perhaps we could afford to ease up on the rituals of march and sit-down. For others, it is possible that the election in 1964 of a Labour Government affected their involvement,

In May 1963 Committee of 100 demonstrators entered RAF Marham in Norfolk to reclaim it for peaceful purposes. Sixty eight were charged under Section 1 of the Official Secrets Act; solidarity action a week later, in which a further 56 people were arrested on the base, led to the substitution of a less serious charge for all of them.

Credit: John Hopkins

either because they now trusted that government to begin the disarmament process, or because they finally despaired of influencing the party which had only had a policy of unilateral nuclear disarmament for one year whilst in opposition. Perhaps a movement sustained by large numbers and persistent campaigning might have affected Labour policy whilst in government, but, in the light of that Government's shameful support for the Vietnam and Biafran wars, I personally doubt it.

Of course the survival of CND as an organisation was of immense value when the movement 'rose again'. While the many stayed at home, there were still those who carried on. More imaginative actions were attempted against nuclear weapons, such as the 'happening' at USAF Alconbury in 1966, when 300 people chanted 'om', planted broken crosses to commemorate the dead of Vietnam, read poetry and burnt banners. (The second part of the 'happening', intended to 'catch the demon of war', was called off when the 'ghost trap' built to effect this feat was blown off the lorry transporting it.)

The same activists took their experience into other campaigns. The formation of the International Confederation for Disarmament and Peace in 1963 signalled a new international awareness. Close links were formed between the Committee of 100 and its newly formed equivalent in Greece. The London Committee of 100 organised demonstrations in 1963 during the London visit of the Greek royal family, in protest against the continued detention of political prisoners and against the recent murder of Greek MP Gregory Lambrakis by agents of the security forces. Good coverage of Greece in *Peace News* in subsequent years helped maintain the connection: when the Colonels' coup occurred in 1967, former members of the Committee of 100 organised a nonviolent occupation of the Greek Embassy in protest. Forty-one people (including two *Peace News* reporters) stood trial at the Old Bailey; three received severe jail sentences.

There was a growing realisation, particularly amongst those influenced by the Committee of 100, that 'banning the bomb' would involve greater social changes, that 'the bomb' was not just a sick excrescence on a healthy body politic, but a symptom of its diseased condition. It was this awareness that helped lead to the development of the concept of nonviolent revolution, a phrase which was to become *Peace News'* subtitle after 1971.

This awareness also led to a concern with trying to make changes locally as well as globally. Indeed, if the policies of the super-powers seemed impervious to peace campaigns, perhaps there were more immediate, if smaller, gains to be made in people's lives. Housing was a particularly important issue: as early as January 1963 the Committee of 100 held an assembly outside a homeless people's hostel, linking the spending on defence to homelessness. Former Committee activists were to be found at the forefront of the revived squatting movement in 1968, applying the techniques of nonviolent direct action to solving the most immediate pressing need for thousands of people — a home.

The '60s were also a time when people turned from trying to prevent an unthinkable future war to trying to stop the all too thinkable wars already taking place. This has always been part of the role of the war resister, of course, whether by protest, by refusing to fight and helping those refusing, or by direct nonviolent intervention. The war in Vietnam had already reached the front page of *Peace News* by May 1963 and it was inevitably to hold that position frequently in the subsequent twelve years. Some of the divisions the anti-war movement would have were apparent from the start. Adam Roberts doubted whether the National Liberation Front would set up an 'independent and free' South Vietnam and suggested a nonviolent alternative to military struggle. But Malcolm Caldwell (a frequent and informative *Peace News* correspondent, despite political differences) thought that such ideas on non-military methods to stop the NLF 'interesting' but that 'the point is that we should be trying to stop the war'.

As the war went on, pacifists found some of the company they kept increasingly uncomfortable: the confrontational demonstrations of the Vietnam Solidarity Campaign were a long way from nonviolent tactics and, for many, the demand to withdraw US troops and end British complicity did not have to involve supporting victory for the NLF. *Peace News* gave coverage and considerable support to the proponents of the Buddhists' Third Way, the nonviolent alternative to the governments of both North and South. The Vietnamese Buddhists were an effective force in many ways, in bringing down the Diem regime in 1963, by their support of draft resistance within Vietnam, and their constructive social service and relief work. But despite their commitment and self-sacrifice, the war ultimately resulted in a defeat for their political approach. For many people, though, the over-riding concern was to get the troops out: David McReynolds of the US War Resisters' League foresaw that 'the Vietnamese were going to make ghastly mistakes after the war', but he believed 'it was their right to make ghastly mistakes'.

Pacifists' initiatives were not lacking. Traditionally, the pacifist position is not simply to protest against wars but to do whatever is possible to get the forces out — one by one if necessary. The public destruction of draft cards and refusal of military service in the USA were already under way when the War Resisters' International (WRI) produced a leaflet addressed to troops, which suggested action they could take if they, too, thought the war was wrong. The action proposed ranged from demonstrations in barracks through registering as conscientious objectors to considering desertion. The movement in Britain, on America's unsinkable aircraft carrier, was well placed to distribute these to US servicemen, and a large number of USAF bases were leafleted at various times.

It was harder to find other forms of direct action. The Nonviolent Action Committee, with 200 demonstrators, blockaded the offices of Elliott Automation (involved in selling aircraft components to the Americans) in 1968, the first time that nonviolent direct action was supported officially by CND. But by and large other protests, though dramatic, were just that — protest. For example, in 1966, members of the Vietnam Action Group and others caused a stir when they interrupted Prime Minister Harold Wilson's reading of the lesson in church at the Labour Party conference, an action which led to several arrests and jail sentences for two people. If war resisters were confined to protest rather than resistance, it may have been because it was much harder to find public acts of real resistance in Britain than in America: the dramatic and effective acts of draft dodging, desertion and acts of nonviolent sabotage, such as the destruction of draft files, were unavailable here. The effectiveness of leafleting individual troops is impossible to calculate; though some US draft resisters and deserters were helped on their way in Britain, the number has, of necessity, not been recorded.

Vietnam was not the only war. *Peace News* was almost alone in exposing the war in Biafra, the extent of famine there and the Wilson government's sale of arms to the Nigerians. There was remarkably little outcry, even from those unions and Labour Party members who had passed a resolution at the previous Party conference to oppose the arms sales the government was now making; an honourable exception was the refusal of dockers in Middlesbrough in January 1969 to load a ship with arms destined for Nigeria. Aid ships, partly sponsored by *Peace News*, set off a little later, but the Nigerians obstructed access to Biafra. Faced with the knowledge that in the aftermath of the Biafran military collapse five million could starve, and evidence that some British troops as well as British arms had gone to Nigeria, the mood was one of despair and shame.

Perhaps the failure to respond adequately to Biafra led to swifter action to try and support the people of Bangladesh. Operation Omega, which was supported by the WRI, was 'not just a mission of relief but an act of interference' and found a ready response in terms of volunteers, money and media coverage, though many volunteers came from outside the peace movement. Omega was perhaps the single most effective pacifist intervention in a recent war: several teams took in food, clothing and medicine whilst others, as an overt political demonstration, set out to challenge the Pakistani army's control of the Indian border with East Pakistan when so many people were starving. After the Indian army's invasion and Bangladesh's declaration of independence, the Biharis became the oppressed community within Bangladesh. Omega turned its attention to them, administering relief, setting up a school and a clinic, and helping to mediate between the Biharis and the reprisals of the Bengalis.

Although Britain has had a fully 'voluntary' army since the discharge of the last conscripts in 1963, the need to support conscientious objectors has remained. Some service people developed objections to continued service because they became opposed to all wars, to a specific war, such as that in Ireland, or to nuclear weapons. For many, the start of their public careers would come with a letter published in *Peace News* declaring their support for nuclear disarmament and proceed, via discipline, to discharge. One was even arrested in the middle of a Vietnam demonstration in 1965 as supporters sat around him trying to prevent military police reaching him. Two soldiers in Aden were arrested in 1964 for printing and distributing Committee of 100 leaflets. Subsequently there have been objectors to the war in Ireland. The course taken by them has varied: some have gone absent without leave or even deserted, while others have become conscientious objectors.

Objection is not just an individual matter, though, and reports of several soldiers' organisations have found their way into *Peace News*. In 1971, a UK-based GI organisation called People Emerging Against Corrupt Establishments (surely the nicest acronym ever) presented the US ambassador with a thousand signature petition against the Vietnam war. Like so many army movements, 'it started off by being a forum for gripes about military life and quickly developed a more political' orientation'. By 1975, *Peace News* was able to report on soldiers' organisations, of varying degrees of radicalism, in France, Italy, Germany, Sweden, Switzerland and the Netherlands. In Britain, despite the efforts of the Soldiers' Charter group, formed in 1971, organisation has been fragmented and quickly suppressed; organising within a non-conscripted army is necessarily more difficult.

Two interviews with Dutch anti-militarists in 1976 high-lighted the differences of approach between those who want nothing to do with armed service and those trying to organise within the forces. The group Onkruit were total resisters: by not registering as conscientious objectors, by refusing 'alternative service' and thus going to jail, they refused to recognise the army at all. On the other hand, BVD was a specifically socialist organisation aiming to 'control the army from inside' by, among other ways, infiltrating the 'official' soldiers' union the Dutch army allowed conscripts to join.

It was not necessary to go round the world, though, to find war and injustice. 'What about *PN* — where does the fight for peace begin for this journal?' a reader asked in 1963, outlining the corrupt system and repressive laws in Northern Ireland. The injustices of Northern Ireland may not have featured much before 1968, but when the Civil Rights movement and People's Democracy began, *Peace News* reporter Kevin McGrath was there. He was there, too, when the civil rights march to Derry was attacked at Burntollet. He predicted that either 'we go forward with "tactical non-violence" . . . to a more radical, subtle and "principled" non-violence . . .. Otherwise it's going to be guns'.

As the war began in earnest, pacifists differed over what action they could take. Several, including *Peace News* co-editors Bob Overy and, later, Robin Percival, felt the right course was to go and live in Northern Ireland; their aim was to help develop activities in the communities they lived in which could lead to reconciliation and change. Their presence there led to well-informed and thoughtful reporting in *Peace News*. Will Warren, a Quaker who lived in Derry for six years, worked to develop trust with paramilitaries in both communities and intervened to save lives. Warren felt (in his assessment of his work in *Peace News*, 12 October 1979) that his relationships in the community, including those with children and his intervention in violent situations, meant that people, 'accepted my sincerity and acknowledged the fact that non-violence does not mean simply opting out of the struggle. It does not mean standing on the sidelines watching others do the work and face the danger.'

Others, including Michael Randle, were more critical of going to live in another community, for fear of seeming patronising; they believed that 'the main task for British radicals is in Britain'. Though a number of pacifists did go, in 1972, to leaflet troops in Northern Ireland with a leaflet produced by the WRI, the feeling that action against the war was needed in *Britain* led to the formation in 1973 of the British Withdrawal from Northern Ireland Campaign (BWNIC). Addressing itself specifically to British civilians and soldiers, it demanded that the Government name a date for withdrawal of troops and that the Union between Britain and Northern Ireland be ended. In its founding statement, 124 supporters pledged their intention to campaign among civilians to this end and to ask soldiers to consider what opposition they could make including, in the final resort, deserting.

Campaigning among civilians, however, was not given the priority that direct contact with soldiers received. Direct contact was a form of direct action and it was also risky — Michael Tobin had been jailed under the Incitement to Disaffection Act the previous year for possessing leaflets addressed to soldiers. Unlike the leafleting of GIs by British civilians, leafleting British squaddies led to arrest and prosecution. In 1974, Pat Arrowsmith spent nine months in jail for distributing BWNIC's 'Some Information for British Soldiers', a leaflet which suggested various ways — both legal and illegal — in which soldiers could leave the army if they had decided to oppose the war in Ireland. Undeterred, BWNIC produced another, modified, leaflet, but this, too, led to court. In a show-piece Old Bailey trial, fourteen supporters, including a *Peace News* co-editor, were accused of conspiring to break the Incitement to Disaffection Act; they were acquitted in December 1975. After their acquittal, charges were dropped against eleven further supporters round the country facing similar charges.

While the trial led to some publicity for the campaign and the acquittal appeared to give a licence for leafleting, it is my opinion as a member of the defence campaign that the energies tied up — necessarily — in a fourteen month process, and the political compromises involved in that defence, both inside and outside court, led to a diminished, more rigid and less libertarian organisation and to its demise a couple of years later.

Peace News was central to the development of the anti-nuclear power movement in Britain in the mid-70s, putting the case against 'civil' nukes and publishing first-hand accounts of actions abroad, such as the nonviolent occupations at Wyhl, Germany, and Seabrook, USA. It acted as a forum for the movement, in particular helping to explain such methods of organising as affinity groups, decentralised decision-making, and training for nonviolent action. With the revival of the nuclear disarmament movement in 1979, it has continued to play an active role in developing those techniques and provides regular coverage of peace camps and nonviolent direct actions.

The nuclear disarmament movement today is undoubtedly larger than it was during the 'first wave' and has already displayed more staying power. There are probably several reasons for this: CND has an organisational structure more democratic than before (though still unwieldy) and is too diverse to be homogenous. There is more emphasis on autonomy within the organisation, as well as a more relaxed relationship with peace groups outside. Disagreements about tactics have not divided the movement, and different approaches can be seen more easily as complementary rather than competitive.

Since 1982 'considered nonviolent direct action' has been CND policy: at a national level direct action has been organised at Burghfield (Easter 1983), Molesworth (February 1985) and organising for Coulport in October 1986 is under way as I write. Direct action by other groups, such as the Greenham Common Women's Peace Camp, has also been given active support by CND.

The diversity of approach is exemplified by the successful

Demonstrators scaling the fence at Molesworth, proposed second Cruise missile base, in March 1986.

Credit: Viv Kendon

struggle by Mid-Glamorgan CND to prevent the construction of a County Wartime Bunker at Bridgend in 1982. Conventional campaigning, a peace camp on the site, the active support of local trade unions and dramatic direct action (with demonstrators sitting on the site as contractors poured concrete over them) culminated in the bunker's cancellation.

The new movement is also better informed on the issues: whereas a critic of CND's 'too intellectual' *Steps Towards Peace* (1962) protested that ordinary campaigners couldn't be expected to argue about 'the merits of nuclear-free zones in Latin America', today's activists certainly can. The movement is also better equipped with techniques. For direct actions, there are attempts to organise in small groups, a network of trainers to help them prepare and full legal briefings and support during demonstrations. There is a full range of campaigning techniques, including some very 'professional' ones like media training and the use of advertising agencies.

Strategically, there has been much greater emphasis on looking for 'transitional' demands, such as the refusal of cruise missiles, cancellation of Trident and the creation of a European nuclear-free zone. (European Nuclear Disarmament, in campaigning for the latter, provided an important impetus to the revival of the movement in 1980.) These are more achievable aims (though none have yet been achieved) than the overall demand to 'ban the bomb', but campaigning for them has sometimes been at the expense of putting the case for complete nuclear disarmament for Britain. There has been less discussion, though, on the strategy for achieving those aims, in particular, how direct action or civil disobedience should be used in a parliamentary democracy. Such actions are often presented as 'obviously' the best thing to do (provided people feel able to risk arrest) with little debate on how, in political terms, their use will lead to disarmament.

There are two aspects of today's movement, though, which seem to me a great advance on twenty years ago. One is the way in which local activists have managed to work successfully with local authorities in the creation of the nuclear-free zone movement. This change in perspective has not been reflected much in *Peace News*, which continues to be suspicious of those who work in or with political parties, even at a local level. But this widespread resistance to 'civil defence', which achieved a notable success when the Government cancelled its 'Hard

Rock' exercise in 1982, is important for local campaigning and its long-term national repercussions.

Secondly, both politically and personally, the flowering of the women's peace movement is of the utmost importance. Women have always been active in the peace movement, and even before the women set up camp at Greenham Common in 1981, there was a specifically women's peace movement. Of course, like other movements, we have our divisions: some believe that women are 'natural peace makers' or have a special role as mothers, while others believe rather that feminists have a particular analysis of militarism and effective ways of working to bring to the struggle for peace. The very right of women to organise *as* women (either separately or in mixed groups) is frequently challenged within the movement. But it seems plain to me that the strength of women within the modern peace movement makes it possible for more women to join, and sustains those, like myself, who have been in it for many years. For the struggle against war and that for a just society are not, and never have been, divisible.

Nonviolent Resistance and Social Defence

by Howard Clark

Pacifist campaigners perennially have to face questions beginning 'What would you do if . . .' and, in particular on defence policy, 'What would you do if the country was invaded?' There are three main types of response. One is that a policy of active peace-making could reduce the likelihood of war — this can be seen as a form of 'preventive pacifism'. In contrast, military preparations — especially nuclear 'defence' — are often provocative and increase the chances of attack. A second line of argument challenges the need for national defence, arguing that governments tend to be more concerned with the defence of privilege than with the defence of people's rights. Existing bosses need resisting now in the same way as would hypothetical invaders. A third type of answer is actually to suggest that nonviolent methods of defence can provide an alternative to military defence and to give historical examples of the success of nonviolence.

All three tendencies can be found in 20th century pacifism in Britain, and each has at times been represented in *Peace News*. Perhaps the dominant tendency in *Peace News* in recent years has been to assert that the means used to disarm and dismantle the warfare State will be the means used to defend a nonviolent society; that a defence policy of nonviolent resistance begins now with defending social groups under attack and defending the whole of humankind against the nuclear threat. This kind of assertion has been made repeatedly in *Peace News*, but generally at the level of rhetoric. This article tries to look critically at the development of this position.

The Failure of 'Preventive Pacifism'

Many of those who have concentrated on 'preventive pacifism' have put their faith in — and much effort into — establishing international institutions — forums where governments could negotiate and debate rationally. Pacifists were active in trying to establish first the League of Nations and later the United Nations as effective instruments of 'international opinion'. Some went further, taking up ideas of world federalism, or looking for a supra-national authority. The failure — especially of the League of Nations — to achieve a world without war brought a profound disillusionment and a questioning of the practicality of a complete renunciation of armed force.

The experience of the Second World War, where small countries were overrun by a great power, strengthened the case for some form of 'collective security'. In the event this led to the formation of military blocs, and 'international order' — after the Yalta agreements drawn up by Roosevelt, Stalin and Churchill — became a matter of the rival superpowers each having its own 'sphere of influence'. The alternative form of collective security, favoured by many with pacifist sympathies, was represented by the United Nations and the hope of some world government.

The idea of world government raised extremely divisive issues for pacifists, almost splitting the major British pacifist organisation — the Peace Pledge Union — in the late 1940s, when its Council unsuccessfully recommended a fundamental change of policy: a switch from rejecting *all* armies to accepting the legitimacy of armed force in the service of a world authority, such as the United Nations, and in enforcing international law. John Middleton Murry, editor of *Peace News* from 1941–46, even argued that the United Nations should be armed with nuclear weapons. Outside the ranks of the PPU, Bertrand Russell — a supporter of World Government — went so far as to suggest in 1948 that, while the US still retained its nuclear monopoly, it should threaten immediate nuclear war against the Soviet Union 'for the purpose of forcing nuclear disarmament upon her'.[1]

Among those who drew a different lesson from the Second World War was Roy Walker, who examined in particular the experience of Norway.[2] Norway's foreign policy of positive neutrality during the 1930s, its commitment to support the League of Nations and its willingness to mediate between the great powers had been almost a model for pacifists. But the Nazi occupation of Norway showed that 'preventive pacifism' by one or two nations could not guarantee their security — Churchill had no more intention than Hitler of respecting Norwegian neutrality. The lesson post-war Norwegian governments drew was to join a military alliance. Despite pursuing generally more enlightened and humanitarian policies than most European states, they have sought security through NATO. Walker, however, saw an alternative logic: a pacifist foreign policy needs to be backed up not by outside protection from the militarily powerful, but by a defence policy of nonviolent resistance.

The Failure of International Solidarity

Moving on to the second line of response — that national defence is actually defending the interests of a specific class — its most influential advocates were the anti-militarist socialists and anarchists before the First World War. Rather than worker killing worker in a quarrel between rulers, the Second International agreed to meet war with an international general strike. When the choice had to be made, however, in 1914, international solidarity in class struggle was found to be a much weaker force than nationalism, and workers were stampeded into a war to kill and be killed by each other. After this, anti-militarism ceased to be a major force within the international socialist movement, despite the efforts of pacifists and anarchists.

In the 1980s, the rhetoric of internationalism from below retains its appeal — especially in the European peace movements' vision of people acting as if boundaries had ceased to exist and engaging in person to person peace-making, 'detente from below'. Yet, as today's anti-nuclear movements seem to recognise, the simple desire for greater security is a more fundamental motivation than internationalism, and in many countries — perhaps, above all, in Britain — the anti-nuclear argument has been popularised more in terms of national safety than of a vision which transcends nations and states.

An Alternative to War

For social change movements to co-operate successfully across frontiers, they need to have a programme which would make sense if it were carried out independently in each local situation. In the absence of an anti-war policy which could be unilaterally implemented in their own country, many First World War

socialists fell into line with the national mood. Some people —
in Britain, Bertrand Russell, for instance — did suggest mass
non-co-operation as a *future* alternative to military defence
against invasion 'after a generation of instruction in the
principles of passive resistance'.[3] But the idea had been neither
sufficiently developed nor widely enough canvassed to be a real
option.

By the 1930s, following the successful general strike against
the Kapp Putsch in Germany (1920) and the nonviolent
resistance to French occupation of the Ruhr (1923),[4] and as
awareness grew of Gandhi's successful experiments with
nonviolent action, there was a stronger current within pacifism
which saw nonviolent resistance as a possible defence policy.
Although the Spanish Civil War forced many pacifists to
abandon their renunciation of all wars as impractical idealism,
the works of the American Quaker, Richard Gregg,[5] and the
Dutch anarchist, Bart de Ligt,[6] persuaded others that there were
effective means of waging conflict which were consistent with
pacifist beliefs.

The idea of meeting an occupier with 'folded arms' and
'fraternisation' gained ground. In retrospect, some of the
writing of '30s pacifists is embarrassing. Wilfred Wellock, for
instance, could not envisage the ruthlessness of the Nazi war
machine. He wrote:

> an invading army being greeted with kindliness and hospitality, and
> a calm refusal to be anyone's slaves, would be wholly unable to
> continue shooting down their hosts in cold blood. (PN, 27.3.37)

Not surprisingly, many pacifists remained sceptical.

Yet the actual experience of occupation indicated that
conquerors are not uniformly unscrupulous, that they rely on
the active co-operation of at least some, and the passive
acquiescence of most of the occupied population, in order to
carry out their policies. In the circumstances, nonviolence was
often the most promising form of resistance. Many European
pacifists were active in the resistance movements, and —
especially after Dunkirk, when fear of invasion of Britain was at
its height — British pacifists, too, looked urgently at techniques
of nonviolent resistance.

Into the Nuclear Age

In the 1950s, inspired by the success of the independence

movement in India and the many instances of nonviolent defiance of Nazi domination, a new interest arose in the technique of nonviolent resistance as a means of defence. The most prolific and well-known exponent of these ideas was and remains Gene Sharp, right from the time he joined the staff of *Peace News* in 1955 to the present.[7]

In the nuclear age, however, not only pacifists saw the potential of nonviolent resistance as a defence policy. Commander Sir Stephen King-Hall and military historian Captain Basil Liddell-Hart were just two of the strategic thinkers who began to take a close interest. King-Hall's personal crusade for a Royal Commission on Unarmed Defence was extensively reported and debated in *Peace News* in the mid-1950s. Editorially, *Peace News* criticised some of the terms in which King-Hall framed his alternative to nuclear deterrence. In particular, where he proposed to mount a massive propaganda campaign against Communism, *Peace News* urged a campaign in support of human rights wherever they were suppressed — East and West. But, in general, the paper in the 1950s was keen to promote nonviolent resistance as an alternative defence policy, a practical policy which could be adopted immediately without wholesale conversions to absolute pacifism or utopian social changes. At the same time, nonviolent direct action was being discussed and practised in real situations — most notably by the emerging anti-H-bomb campaign in Britain and the civil rights movement in the US.

Effectiveness of Nonviolence

Often war and violence are presented as a last resort — war after the failure of diplomacy, violence after the failure of peaceful protest. Yet often nonviolent tactics and strategy have been adopted pragmatically, as either the only possibility or the most effective form of action. Nonviolent movements have then grown up less out of pacifist principle than because other means offer no hope. This was the case with the US civil rights movement.

Although in the late 1940s and early 1950s pacifists had been active in the 'freedom rides' to de-segregate inter-state buses in the US, when Bayard Rustin — a Black field worker for the US War Resisters' League — went down to Alabama in 1956 at the beginning of the Montgomery bus boycott, he found:

> not one of the Negro leaders in Montgomery was a pacifist when the

struggle began . . . When we present the total impact of pacifist philosophy . . . we may be asking the impossible. It is important for us to learn to create situations within which they can learn by doing. The *strategy* of nonviolence ought to be greatly emphasised. The principle of nonviolence will be accepted only when the strategy has been adopted. (PN, 25.10.57)

Rustin proceeds to tell a story of how some young blacks learnt by doing:

> We called together the most violent young men, not to tell them it was not nice to have and use guns, but to point out the immediate social consequences of having them. It was a strategic discussion. We developed a technique of involving them in the core of the nonviolent struggle. About a thousand bicycles had been collected all over the State and sent to Montgomery and parked in a large field. We persuaded these young men . . . to protect these bikes without violence. They did so, and were finally prepared to dump their guns in the river.

(The one question overlooked in the strategic discussion was 'what would have ensued had the police caught us on that drive to the river, in possession of a truck load of weapons'!)

In Britain, pacifists were central to the embryonic anti-nuclear weapons movement. They were discovering the effectiveness of nonviolent tactics in arousing a public debate which the machinery of government had been determined to avoid. At the same time, they sensed the potential of nonviolent resistance as a defence strategy. Tony Weaver, who took part in the direct action at the Thor missile base at Swaffham in 1958, wrote to *Peace News* commenting:

> Events at Swaffham have suggested that nonviolent resistance against this country's war preparations could provide a training ground now for the mass use of this weapon against an invader. For those whose minds think in terms of a deterrent, this could become a real alternative to the nuclear one, and a more realistic training than Civil Defence which lulls people into a false sense of security. (30.1.59)

Weaver's hope has been reiterated many times, in the pages of *Peace News* and elsewhere. Yet since the 1950s there has been a growing divergence in Britain between the practitioners of nonviolent action and those seeking to promote it as an alternative to military defence.

Where the 1930s advocates of nonviolent resistance were

explicitly pacifist — Gregg relating nonviolent action to a moral philosophy and De Ligt to social revolution — in the late 1950s and early 1960s, *Peace News* writers such as Adam Roberts and Gene Sharp increasingly sought to divorce nonviolent resistance from pacifist philosophy.

Adam Roberts — who was on the staff of *Peace News* from 1962 to 1965 — felt a need to debunk some of the religiosity and moralism around nonviolence:

> A belief in nonviolent action is often taken to mean a religious or utopian attitude (the devotees of which hold 'witnesses') or else a minority obstructionist attitude typified by some of the actions of the Committee of 100. I think nonviolent action should be seen as a weapon which can be used as a means of preserving our society and our values without involving the risk of mutual destruction in thermonuclear war. (PN 10.5.63)

Because it was unrealistic to expect agreed, multilateral disarmament, Roberts argued that unilateralism required a viable, disarmed defence policy. He repeatedly criticised the Campaign for Nuclear Disarmament for failing to offer hope. Instead of simply asking people to renounce existing defence policy, CND should make nonviolent defence a major part of its platform.

How could such a defence policy be introduced? Here Roberts fell out with the activists. As a colleague on *Peace News* — features editor Michael Freeman — put it, Roberts and Sharp were offering nonviolent resistance as 'top people's defence', to be introduced by the political and even military establishment, rather than won from below. Freeman's review of the 1964 *Peace News* pamphlet *Civilian Defence*[8] was trenchant. He warned that this theory:

> could turn out to be a reactionary one: by emphasising national unity, it plays down the importance of internal social struggle; by emphasising nationalistic nonviolence, it ignores the international character of organised violence (military alliances, cartels, etc) . . . My own view is that, if revolutionary nonviolent action is ever to be generally adopted, it must grow out of people's present concerns. People have problems enough, without adding the hypothetical ones of invasion and coup d'etat. If they can be helped to resist the injustice they face now in their own lives by taking action themselves, in alliance not with the Government or the military but with those who have common cause with them in fighting this injustice, then the basis for a mass movement of nonviolent direct action might be formed (PN, 13.3.64).

A key function of the Resistance in Europe against Nazi occupation was the dissemination of information. Here a Danish dental clinic was converted into a composing room; it could be restored at a moment's notice, with the typesetters becoming the dentist and his patients.

Roberts replied that there was no necessary connection between pursuing nonviolent action for social justice or domestic causes and developing a policy of nonviolent defence. Gandhian nonviolence in India in the cause of independence and social change had not provided an alternative to military means of waging international conflict. Indeed, at the time of the Sino-Indian border conflict, most 'Gandhians' in India, including Gandhi's 'spiritual heir' Vinoba Bhave, had rallied behind their government and army just as readily as most First World War socialists put national interest before class interest.

Increasingly, the Roberts-Sharp circle hoped that the ideas of civilian resistance as a defence policy would gain acceptance in military circles. Sharp, from having been one of the mentors of the anti-nuclear civil disobedients of the 1950s, by the 1980s downplays the role of the peace movement and seems to believe that nonviolent direct action against military policies is more likely to hinder than promote the adoption of civilian defence. Sharp's political trajectory — from campaigning politics to putting his faith in the willingness of the military and governments to listen to expert advice — bears out the warnings of some of his 1960s critics.

In 1967, *Peace News* co-editor Bob Overy used the occasion of the publication of *The Strategy of Civilian Defence*[9] to attack the 'nonviolence salesmen'. Contributors to the book included *Peace News* writers such as Roberts himself, Sharp, Theodore Ebert and April Carter. They drew on the history of nonviolent resistance to the Nazis and to totalitarian Communist rule to present nonviolent action as a credible alternative defence policy which did not require a philosophy of nonviolence or a commitment to pacifism. Overy denounced this as a diversion from the pacifist's real purpose of developing nonviolence as a strategy for transforming a war-making society. Commenting on the debate 11 years later, he reiterated his position:

> What I object to is civilian defence as a half-way house, in which the attempt is made to strip nonviolence of much of its radical content in order to make it acceptable to the powers-that-be . . . The two basic points of my article still stand for me. First, civilian defence aims to convert the wrong groups in society to nonviolent action. There is no short cut. Our priority should be to build a nonviolent revolutionary movement which will radically transform the institutions and practices of our society. Second, we should not permit nonviolence to be stripped of its positive spiritual and social content.[10]

This episode in 1967 virtually ended the debate in *Peace News* — apart from brief flurries of interest in 1973 and 1977. Instead, arguments shifted to the effectiveness of nonviolence as a form of protest or as a means of social change.

Nonviolence on the Defence

By the late 1960s, with the rise of the Vietnam Solidarity Campaign, advocates of nonviolent protest were on the defensive in Britain and elsewhere. For many on the left, in the student and 'underground' movements, the term 'nonviolence' was discredited. When Che Guevara died in Bolivia, he was seen not as the victim of a futile attempt to export a Cuban model of revolution, but as a romantic hero. In the US, urban Blacks rioted and militants denounced the compromises of Martin Luther King and armed themselves. The Tet Offensive in Vietnam showed the world that the military might of the US could be defeated. And when, in Paris in May 1968, a student revolt threatened to bring down De Gaulle, a revolution catalysed by youth and students throughout the Western world seemed on the agenda.

The contagion spread to Northern Ireland, where the civil rights movement and its radical student wing, People's Democracy, challenged the discrimination inherent in that society. Their nonviolent protests opened up new possibilities of change, but this nonviolence could not be sustained in the face of fierce loyalist reaction.

By 1970, it had become impossible to organise a large, nonviolent peace demonstration in Britain. When the US invaded Cambodia, despite all the efforts of the organisers, the march degenerated inevitably into a clash between a section of the demonstrators and the police. Although the Stop the Seventy Tour campaign against links with apartheid sport, explicitly called for nonviolent action, fighting broke out on most of its demonstrations.

Anti-racism, Anti-fascism

One of the most difficult arenas of activity for white people committed to nonviolence in 1970s was anti-racism and anti-fascism. Here street-fighting macho rode high. Several groups tried to find nonviolent responses which did not rely on the machinery of State or on a Smash the Fash mentality. The

Manchester Gay Libertarians in 1974 argued that:

> the main strategy of opposition must be through involving people
> in their everyday situations, both at work and in the community;
> through women's groups, black groups, gay groups organising
> themselves; by coherent libertarian politics which cease to split the
> 'personal' from the 'political' and which reject *all* authority,
> whether from the right or the 'left'. (PN, 4.1.74)

The Birmingham Counter-Fascist Group took this further in its
1976 pamphlet on an alternative approach to countering
fascism. This urged whites to 'get in touch with our own
(internal) "fascist" . . .. Nonviolence is about learning to
communicate with our own worst selves.' Such an approach led
two years later to a *Peace News* pamphlet, *Taking Racism
Personally* whose principal editors were Brenda Thompson and
Keith Paton, one of the prime movers of the Birmingham
Group.

In Bradford, the Manningham Defence committee — a
predominantly white group consisting of gays, feminists,
counter-culture types and some students at the Bradford School
of Peace Studies — called a 'carnival sit-down', at which 129
people were arrested in June 1976. Its style was consciously
nonviolent — an attempt to show that 'it is possible to have fun
and be positive and peaceful when making a political point'.
(Unlike the Birmingham group, however, it also looked for State
action to 'enforce the Race Relations Act — ban the NF'.)

Having an overwhelmingly white readership and feeling on
the periphery of anti-racist, anti-fascist activity, *Peace News* —
not for the first time — lacked a social base for developing
nonviolent strategies. It therefore had to fall back on reprints,
on experience from elsewhere (usually from the US), and on
imagination. When, in 1976, it reprinted an account from *Race
Today* of an evening patrol in East London by an Asian vigilante
group in cars, *Peace News* supported Black people's right to self-
defence, but warned of the dangers of escalation. It also referred
back to a 1973 article about a strategy adopted in Philadelphia to
make the streets safer — a community walk,[11] which not only
involved women more but helped build more community
feeling. After the battle of Lewisham in 1977, when the police
tried to clear a route for a National Front march which anti-
fascists and the local community were trying to block, *Peace
News* printed a fantasy about 'Mashiwel', in which in similar
circumstances, the local community decided not to confront the

National Front but to 'cold shoulder' them by shutting up shop for the day — a nonviolent tactic successfully employed by Catholics in Dungiven in 1969 when Loyalists marched through.

Pat Arrowsmith was one of the few pacifists involved in the summer of 1978 in countering the National Front's use of a corner of Brick Lane, East London, as a base for attacks on local Bengalis. After the first sit-down by Asians, Blacks and white anti-fascists in Brick Lane, Pat Arrowsmith criticised the timidity of many pacifists in discussing responses to the National Front, and in particular the idea that nonviolent action against the National Front *necessitated* intensive nonviolence training.

> If people with a commitment to nonviolence are serious, then rather than sitting back thinking 'only we can do it', we should be out joining in such events, with nonviolence; by helping encourage the one, we spread the other. (PN, 28.7.78)

Others active in anti-fascist work were less optimistic. Sophie Laws and I were stewards on a 'nonviolent' counter-demonstration to the National Front in York where Socialist Workers not only threw sexist taunts at the National Front, but had to be physically restrained from trying to attack them. Even though the Front threw stones at us, we succeeded in curbing any physical retaliation. Laws observed that this was seen as 'imposing our "womanly", "poofy" nonviolence on them [SWP]'. My report concluded:

> on counter-demonstrations to the NF, we don't have much choice but to secure people's agreement to nonviolence, and get [factional] minorities to stick to it, or to stay out of united fronts dominated by street-fighting men . . .
>
> But is it worth the effort? It's difficult enough to have a nonviolent demonstration of any sort which will communicate with rather than antagonise non-participants, let alone having to tame the SWP as well. And how can we begin to raise questions about fascism — questions about masculinity, women's oppression, sexual repression, authoritarianism and the family — when working with 'comrades' who glory in their manliness? (PN, 21.10.77)

Training, Affinity Groups and Anti-nuclear Energy

From 1969 to 1971, George Lakey and Lynne Shivers from the Philadelphia Life Centre enthused many British pacifists with the methods of nonviolence training. This promised to help us regain their capacity to organise more ambitious nonviolent protest. Initially, training focused very much on how to be able to carry through an action nonviolently — both responding nonviolently to police provocation and restraining violent elements among the protesters. But training also tried to provide structures of support for activists, where — in the safety of a 'role-play' — they could test their reactions and anticipate problems which might crop up in a situation.

The first apostle of 'training for peace' in Britain had been Richard Gregg, another American Quaker. His 1936 pamphlet *Training for Peace*[12] concentrated on building up group morale through singing, folk-dancing and manual work, as well as personal and group understanding through study sessions, readings and meditations. The 1970s training was also a product of its time, featuring co-operative games, including trust and sensitivity exercises taken from encounter groups. The key word became 'empowerment'. But the emphasis of training sessions was less on individual preparedness for action than on the group — improving group decision-making processes, building group spirit, sharing skills and experiences, making sure that every voice in a group was heard, and countering patterns of domination which many groups take for granted — for instance, domination by the more self-confident, articulate, experienced members and by men. However, in the absence of a protest movement committed to nonviolence, pacifists were on the margins, and there was little demand for nonviolence training until the late 1970s when, following the Windscale Inquiry, the British anti-nuclear energy movement turned to nonviolent direct action.

Peace News had been reporting nonviolent action against nuclear power from around Europe since the occupation of Wyhl, West Germany in 1974, and *Peace News* co-editor Mike Holderness had taken part in the traumatic 1977 demonstration at Malville when French riot police killed one demonstrator and maimed four others. At the same time as Mike Holderness was analysing how events at Malville had taken their disastrous turn, other *Peace News* contributors — Sheryl Crown, Martin Jelfs, Peter Jones and Jo Somerset — wrote of their extraordinary experience at the first US occupation of a nuclear power site, Seabrook. The Clamshell Alliance which occupied Seabrook functioned through a system of 'affinity groups', small groups each of which trained for nonviolent action and each of which appointed a spokesperson to take part in Alliance decision-making. Here, it seemed, was a form of organisation which could maintain nonviolence and at the same time encourage participation in decision-making.

In 1978, the Torness Alliance adopted a similar framework for its campaign to stop construction of a nuclear reactor on the Scottish coast, 30 miles from Edinburgh. The nuclear energy question touched many groups involved more in creating an alternative society than in campaigning politics, in particular wholefood shops. For some, the Torness Alliance was almost a crusade for nonviolence — not just in terms of nonviolent action tactics, but in terms of the vision of a nuclear-free, ecologically-sound society. Torness introduced many people both to nonviolence training and to the notion of organising large actions via 'affinity groups'. This in turn provided a base of experience on which CND and anti-missiles activity was to build in the 1980s.

Nonviolence training has helped groups function more effectively, giving us a greater sense of control over our actions in larger demonstrations and greater clarity about our purpose. It has also helped many of us feel supported in our struggle for change, affirmed in our activities, and encouraged in our vision. But training, as it now takes place in Britain, has severe limits. For large nonviolent actions, 'training' too often means 'briefing' — simply relaying essential information about the plan of action and the law, doing little to develop the group taking action or to deepen understanding of nonviolence. At the other end, it often happens that the deeper people get into training, the less do they engage in social struggle; protracted training sessions often attract people whose priority is personal growth and therapy rather than social action. The rhetoric may be about 'empowerment', but the practice can actually involve becoming estranged from people with whom you want to connect.

Nonviolent Action As Social Defence

Since the revival of CND, the concept of 'alternative defence' has largely been of non-nuclear military options. Peace researchers in many countries have continued to investigate the possibilities of nonviolent defence, but the dominant tendencies within the nuclear disarmament movements have looked more to notions of 'defensive deterrence' and 'non-provocative defence' — in short, proposals more likely than nonviolent defence to be acceptable to social-democratic politicians seeking power. The stress is on 'credible', 'genuine', 'real' defence in a way which appears to offer phoney guarantees of security and to evade the disarmament campaigner's central problem of shifting popular values so that most people would rather be vulnerable to attack than to threaten mass annihilation of others.[13]

People committed to nonviolence, however, have tried to connect nonviolent action as a form of protest with nonviolent action as a defence policy. The core concept is *social defence*. Social defence does not assume a national framework, but a framework of social struggle: protecting the environment, upholding certain values, defending a particular institution or people's rights. Its focus is not on what threats might arise, but on immediate situations. In this perspective, the occupations of Elizabeth Garrett Anderson Hospital, London (1975–76) and Thornton View, Bradford (1983–85) were instances of social defence, as are work-ins (defending jobs) and strikes.

Some groups have made an explicit connection between 'social defence' now and alternatives to military national defence. In 1985 *Peace News* adapted a broadsheet on Social Defence first produced in 1980 by Canberra Peacemakers, a group whose activities and perspective are expounded in Brian Martin's book *Uprooting War*.[14] They sought to connect with industrial workers; with groups concerned about community security and street safety, such as feminists; with groups which are targets for public hostility or repression, such as lesbians and gays. At the same time, looking to the future, they held workshops — including one with a community radio station — to draw up contingency plans for responses to a coup or the situation which occurred in Australia in 1975 when the Governor-General intervened to overturn the Whitlam Government.

Aldrig Mere Krig — the Danish Section of War Resisters' International — was invited to draw up a nonviolent defence strategy for Christiania, a 'free city' squatted in a former army barracks in Copenhagen. The women of Christiania decided to take the lead:

> They trust their own self-discipline more than they trust the men, and want to show that Christiania is women with children (60

Nonviolent direct action — a six-month continuous blockade of farmland at Luxulyan in Cornwall — prevented the Central Electricity Generating Board from conducting test drilling for a nuclear power station. A 'captive' drilling rig is shown here in June 1981. Eventually the CEGB abandoned its plans for Luxulyan.

Credit: Mike Wall

children, more than 30 born there) and homes, not tumbledown houses with drug addicts. At the same time, they mean to use the sexist prejudices of society against the authorities. (PN, 6.2.76)

When Christiania finally 'fell', about four years later, it was more as a result of internal collapse and drug abuse than of police action.

The Dutch group Women for Social Defence[15] has incorporated a hand in a halt sign into their symbol. This adapts the anti-racist 'Ne touche pas mon pote' ('Hands off my buddy') badge widely worn in continental Europe and which they see as one form of social defence. The group's first discussions were pooling their experience about occasions when they had stood up for themselves; their first public action was to join a peace camp as an act of defence against cruise missiles.

In Britain in the 1980s, anti-nuclear nonviolent direct action has several stories of successful social defence: in 1981, preventing test-drilling at a possible nuclear power station site at Luxulyan in Cornwall; in 1982, stopping the construction of a bunker at Bridgend; forcing Britain to abandon the dumping of nuclear waste at sea by repeated nonviolent direct action by the Severnside Alliance and Greenpeace, culminating in 1983 with non-co-operation by the rail and sea unions. But let's be clear about the role of the activists in these victories. The key to success was that they catalysed other groups — the whole community around Luxulyan, even the police; the local authority and unions at Bridgend; and on sea-dumping, the International Maritime's Organisation moratorium was crucial in securing union support for the ban.[16]

Lynne Jones has written about Greenham as a form of social defence.[17] Its keynotes are flexibility and improvisation — precisely the qualities which would be needed in the event of military invasion or occupation. I doubt that Greenham women would have been so effective without practical support from central CND, or without the experience many women have had in small group actions and even in nonviolence training, but Lynne contrasts their spontaneity:

> with the established view of nonviolent action which is seen to require a high degree of centralised organisation — with briefings and information beforehand, lengthy preparation in advance for every participant, a lot of time spent on the group process. We have found these methods are too cumbersome to deal with a situation that changes every day.

This analysis could be expanded. One remarkable feature of Greenham is the relationship between the relatively few women camping at any one time and popular mobilisation: 'Greenham women are everywhere', as the slogan says. Thousands of women have descended on the site for mass actions; hundreds of people have visited regularly with wood, food and other supplies; many have taken Greenham home — either by doing actions where they live or sometimes, literally, into their own home and relationships. The women at the camp have had a prophetic role: their absolute and fundamental rejection of patriarchal violence and their determination to celebrate their womanhood, no matter what abuse is heaped on them, has inspired and energised women around the world who find themselves in more conventional circumstances.

Strategy Against Occupation

Analysts of nonviolent defence think of an occupied society as having three components — a tiny minority of active collaborators, a larger and heroic minority of determined resisters, and the great mass of the population, loath to take risks but ardently wishing to end the occupation. A good strategy then seeks (a) to establish structures capable of co-ordinating resistance and withstanding repression; (b) to isolate the collaborators; (c) to find ways by which the majority can deny the occupier's objectives without much risk, and (d) to build up the people's courage. The plan is to frustrate, weaken and ultimately undermine the occupier.

Although the imagery of nonviolent resistance tends to be of general strikes, mass demonstrations, civilians — unarmed and open-handed, or perhaps bearing a flower — approaching a soldier, those. are only the most dramatic moments of resistance. Such a 'nonviolent blitzkrieg' (Sharp's term) may be appropriate as an immediate reaction to invasion, but all-out non-co-operation cannot be sustained indefinitely. Ways are needed to hamper administration and paralyse certain industries which do not call for such open defiance. Against a prolonged occupation, a strategy of attrition and 'semi-resistance' (Michael Randle's term)[18] is often the order of the day. This includes such activities as deliberately misunderstanding orders, making mistakes, going slow. By such means, Danish shipbuilders managed to delay construction of a German warship until after the war had finished. In December 1956 in Hungary, when factory representatives from the Beljanif Electric Works were arrested, their colleagues held a 3-day sit-in strike. They were forced to resume work, the police and militia were posted throughout the factory. Yet even in the face of this intimidation, a mixture of go-slow tactics and poor quality work succeeded in reducing output to 8% of normal production.[19]

Against occupation, existing institutions often provide a basis for resistance — trade unions and churches, especially — and existing political leaders, even if they are in exile or in prison, play an important role. Existing culture will also be mobilised in the cause of resistance — 'culture' here includes the deep-rooted political values of a society as well as religious services, national statues or, as in occupied Denmark, patriotic folk-songs. An 'underground' — pirate radios, clandestine presses, a complete and autonomous system of support and communications — will begin to function parallel to the existing administration, and ready to take over when the occupier is forced to withdraw.

Some of the elements of a strategy against occupation will also be found in other social struggles. Any movement challenging existing power structures needs to be under-pinned by its own counter-structures and its own culture. Morale is a vital factor. Gene Keyes[20] has argued that the 'centre of gravity' of unarmed resistance to occupation is morale, and morale hinges on a sense of power to effect change and also on a steadfast commitment to principles which are felt to be worth dying for.

Strategies also have to accommodate different levels of commitment. There is something that each person can contribute and so a strategy has to have several layers, each offering particular forms of involvement and each reinforcing the others. Thus, while some people will stay up all night or expose themselves to great risks, others will try to introduce some form of resistance into an otherwise routine daily life — for instance, a consumer boycott.

Nonviolent activists would do well to pay attention to these strategic insights, but our own situation is more complicated than resisting military occupation. The immediate focus of nonviolence is social change. A thoroughgoing nonviolence seeks to challenge all forms of domination and to encourage people to grow beyond them. It therefore implies a critique of some of the institutions around which resistance to military occupation would mobilise — not only the Royal Family and the State, but also white, male-dominated, hierarchical organisations such as trade unions and churches. Nonviolence aims to embody the values of the society it wants to bring into being — values which are often fundamentally in conflict with the prevalent culture. The problem is, however, that pacifists often have difficulty in relating the principled commitment to nonviolence with everyday reality — the oppressions and injustices, the frustrations and aspirations — that gives rise to struggle.

Gandhi was clear about the first duty of 'satyagrahis' — core nonviolent activists. It was to propagate the 'constructive programme'. For him, the basis of a non-co-operation campaign had to be this programme. It was directed not only at economic self-reliance — for instance through hand-spinning, wearing handspun cloth, or 'bread labour' (working to feed yourself) — but at social reform. In particular, this involved promoting Hindu-Muslim unity, ending discrimination against women and untouchables, improving sanitation and education.

Explicitly nonviolent movements in Britain have rarely succeeded in combining resistance with a constructive programme grounded in local needs. At a personal level, how do we balance our commitment to make social change with our needs for support and fulfilment? It is all too easy to settle for a 'personal solution', a way of life which may suit us, but which may actually divorce us from a wider struggle. At a collective level, today there is a diverse culture of radical alternatives — rural and inner city, black, feminist, gay and youth — but we are far from seeing what Keith (Paton) Motherson called for in 1977:

> autonomous coalitions created by women, centrally, and by gay, black, old, young and disabled people, claimants, freaks and low-paid and public sector workers (PN, 2.12.77).

It is through the excluded, the oppressed and the disaffected connecting with each other that people will grow from claiming their own rights to asserting the rights of all. An effective nonviolent struggle has to go even one step further — in propagating its values and constructing alternatives, it also has to cultivate an empathy with people not yet with us — with the insecure, the scared and the trapped.

1. Bertrand Russell, *The Autobiography of Bertrand Russell*, Unwin Books, 1975 p. 508.

2. Roy Walker, *A People Who Loved Peace*, Victor Gollancz, 1946.

3. Bertrand Russell, 'War and Non-Resistance', *Atlantic Monthly*, 1915, quoted in Michael Randle, 'Aspects of the Debate in Britain on Civilian Defence', paper for the Strasbourg Symposium on Civilian Defence, November 1985.

4. For reading on the Kapp Putsch, see Anders Boserup and Andrew Mack, *War Without Weapons*, Frances Pinter, 1974, pp 122–127, and Gene Sharp, *The Politics of Nonviolent Action*, Porter Sargent, 1973, pp 40–41. On the Ruhrkampf, see Boserup and Mack, pp 92–102, Wolfgang Sternstein, 'The Ruhrkampf of 1923, in Adam Roberts (ed), *The Strategy of Civilian Defence*, Faber and Faber, 1967, pp 106–135.

5. In particular, Richard Gregg, *The Power of Nonviolence*, 1st edition 1935, 2nd revised edition with Foreword by Martin Luther King, James Clarke & Co 1960.

6. Bart de Ligt, *The Conquest of Violence: an essay on war and revolution*, George Routledge & Sons, 1937.

7. Gene Sharp, *The Politics of Nonviolent Action* (3 vols), Porter Sargent, 1973; *Social Power and Political Freedom*, Porter Sargent, 1980; *Making Europe Unconquerable: the potential of civilian-based deterrence and defence*, Taylor & Francis, 1985.

8. Adam Roberts and Gene Sharp (eds), *Civilian Defence* Peace News pamphlet, 1964.

9. Adam Roberts (ed), *The Strategy of Civilian Defence*, Faber and Faber, 1967, revised as Adam Roberts (ed), *Civilian Resistance as a National Defence* Penguin 1969.

10. *Studies in Nonviolence* No 4, Peace Pledge Union, August 1978.

11. Jackie Schirn, 'Good Neighbours in Philadelphia', *Peace News*, 23.3.73.

12. Richard Gregg, *Training for Peace*, Peace Pledge Union, 1936.

13. For a critique of proposals for conventional defensive deterrence, see Howard Clark 'Non-Nuclear Defence: no easy options' in *Genuine Defence* (possibly forthcoming from CND), originally published as 'Disarmament means disarmament', *Peace News*, 13.7.84.

14. Brian Martin, *Uprooting War*, Freedom Press, 1984

15. Women for Peace, National group on social defence, c/o PO Box 363, 3800 AZ Amersfoort, the Netherlands.

16. For short accounts, see Howard Clark, Sheryl Crown, Angela McKee and Hugh MacPherson, *Preparing for Nonviolent Direct Action*, Peace News/CND, 1984; for the Bridgend story, see Tony Simpson, *No Bunkers Here*, Peace News/Mid-Glamorgan CND, 1982

17. Lynne Jones, 'Peaceful Defence', *Sanity*, December 1984.

18. See Chapter 7, 'Defence by Civil Resistance' in the Alternative Defence Commission, *Defence Without the Bomb*, Taylor & Francis, 1983.

19. Andy Anderson, *Hungary '56* Solidarity London 1956, Black and Red Detroit, 1975, p 105.

20. Gene Keyes, 'Strategic Non-violent Defense: the Construct of an Option', *Journal of Strategic Studies* 4, 2 (June 1981), pp 125–51.

To Live Our Lives So As To Take Away The Occasion For War: Some Observations On The Peaceful Economy

by Tom Woodhouse

I. Pacifism and the Principles of the Peaceful Economy

For a long time pacifists have sought to identify the conditions of violence in the economic, social, and political relationships of our society. Nuclear proliferation and the conventional arms race are seen to be symptoms of a society whose economic relationships are fundamentally based on conflict, exploitation, and violence. The value of conventional arms sales doubled from $9.4 billion in 1969 to $19.1 billion in 1978,[1] and the scale and threat of this trade should not be underestimated — it is at least as destabilising as the nuclear arms race, and emanates from 'needs' and absurdities generated within the economies of the western world. Wilfred Wellock, writing in *Peace News* (20 January 1956) put the point simply and well:

> Our economy is a war-producing economy. I am not interested in any disarmament policy which takes no account of basic causative factors.

Wellock, a pacifist and socialist who had become deeply influenced by the ideas of Gandhi, represented a tradition of dissent which attributed the causes of war and of escalating arms production to the key feature of modern industrial culture — the exploitation of people and resources in the pursuit of material abundance. Wellock wished to

> restore the right of every nation to achieve a reasonably self-sufficient economy, and to the people of every nation, including our own, the right to responsibility, creative opportunity, and the vital relationships of a well integrated, organic society.[2]

It follows that the passing of disarmament resolutions at political conferences, although undeniably important, cannot be taken as sufficient for cultivating the conditions of peace. Wellock argued this case in *Peace News* (26 October 1960) in an article entitled 'The First Need is a Non-violent Economy', where he drew out the logic of the Labour Party conference decision of 1960 in favour of unilateral disarmament.

There is not space in this article to discuss the theories which explain the function of military production in capitalist and industrial societies. The literature is vast, but a very good account of the American military, the power house of the world's conventional and nuclear arsenal, is given in the work of Seymour Melman. Melman has argued that a 'permanent war economy' emerged in the USA after 1945, in the form of a military industrial complex (MIC). This MIC in turn became incorporated as a new state management system, controlled by the Pentagon. What characterises the American economy is neither a system of private enterprise, nor even a system of state capitalism, but a state-managed war economy of unprecedented power and capacity.[3]

Any country wishing to disarm significantly must undergo a fundamental re-orientation of the principles of its economic life. If Britain, for example, decided to leave the military orbit of the superpowers, it would be necessary for the country to prepare to withdraw from the international competition for raw materials and markets. As other countries throughout the world raced to industrialise, those with a heavy export dependency would find the competition more severe. The only way out of this competitive spiral would be to reduce international investments: to reduce the levels of arms production and of defence commitments overseas; and to accept a change of national status, no longer assuming the mantle of a great power.

Such a significant adjustment would mean that Britain would have to withdraw from its increasingly desperate competition to sell arms abroad. Along with other major producers like France, Germany, and more recently China, Britain has cut the joint share of the world arms trade held by the Soviet Union and the United States from 80% in 1980, to 62% in 1984. Between 1978 and 1982 the UK had major arms contracts with the following countries:

Table 1: Markets for UK Arms Exports, 1978–82[4]
(UK share of arms import expenditure)

Country	UK Share of Market
Barbados	100
Oman	84
Zimbabwe	67
Brazil	61
Qatar	59
Finland	52
Malawi	50
Guyana	50
Sri Lanka	50
USA	45
Ireland	44
France	44
China	42
Botswana	40
Jordan	35
Honduras	33
Upper Volta	33
Uganda	29
Kuwait	23
Kenya	23
Saudi Arabia	20

(NB. During this period the UK exported weapons to 67 different countries; table 1 lists only those countries where the UK had at least a 20% share of the market of arms imported.)

Pacifists have steadfastly believed that the gain from changing these military industrial priorities would be worthwhile. Wilfred Wellock suggested that Britain would become a

> new magnetic spiritual pole amidst the uncontrollable frenzy of a fear-ridden, power-drunk world, (while gaining) the freedom to develop friendly, co-operative relations with her neighbours to the ends of the earth . . .. But the greatest benefit that would or could follow the adoption of a non-aggressive economy is the emergence of a social order of a finer culture . . . we should be able to decentralise the populations of most of our industrial cities into smallish communities . . . It is in the small community that true democracy finds its maximum opportunity. (PN, 26 October 1960)

This comment of Wellock's echoes a recurrent theme in radical and pacifist writing — the desire to establish a democratic and peaceful economy. Throughout history there has been a tension between large-scale and top-heavy forms of economic organisation on the one hand, and patterns of small-scale association on the other.

Lewis Mumford has referred to this as conflict between two types of system: an 'authoritarian technics', centralised and powerful but inherently unstable; and a 'democratic technics', relatively weak, but resourceful and durable, and based on people's skills.[5]

The domination within the world economy, east and west, of many of the characteristics of the authoritarian technics described by Mumford has resulted in the emergence of an economy of violence, in which the following elements dominate:

* large-scale production, hierarchically and bureaucratically controlled;
* high levels of conflict over possession of the world's resources, and over distribution of rewards for production;
* a complex of military interests in industry and the economy, and the domination of the economic life of towns, localities, regions, and national economies by defence production and military research and development;
* mass-production, standardisation, and the destruction of skills and autonomy;
* a high demand for energy to fuel the industrial machine, and pollution and exploitation of the environment.

By contrast, a peaceful economy would be one where the following characteristics and principles prevailed:

* democratic control and co-operative working patterns;
* a diversity of modes of economic activity, placing primary emphasis on human-centred organisation and on meaningful work;
* production of arms forming a small part of economic activity;
* security based on a conception of defence far wider than a dependence on technology (weapons);
* low levels of violence within and between societies, and the availability of skills and resources to constructively resolve the conflicts which do occur;
* a regard for finite resources and the delicate balance of the environment;

* an awareness of the global consequences of economic activity.

II. Social Movements and the Peaceful Economy

There is a great deal of experience in pacifist history, often reflected in the pages of *Peace News*, which illuminates ways in which these principles of a peaceful economy might become more prevalent, and how a variety of groups have struggled over the centuries to bring out new forms of peaceful economic relationships. The practice of peacemaking and peacebuilding calls into play a number of skills, conceptual and practical. One important role is for the visionaries, the people capable of providing an imaginative and inspirational view of how we might live well. There is much in the tradition of radical pacifism and socialist pacifism on which to draw. It was during the upheavals of the middle years of the seventeenth century that two important traditions emerged. Firstly, the Levellers and the Diggers were the initiators of a radical democratic activity seeking to establish the principles of harmony, co-operation and justice in political and economic relations. At a time when social and political relations generally were in turmoil, and the passions released by the English Civil War at their height, the Digger Gerrard Winstanley eloquently declared his belief in the values of the co-operative commonwealth:

> In the beginning of Time, the Great Creator Reason, made the earth to be the Common Treasury, to preserve Beasts, Birds, Fishes and Man, the lord that was to Govern this creation; for Man and Domination given to him, over the Beasts, Birds, and Fishes; but not one word was spoken in the beginning. That one branch of mankind should rule over another.
>
> And the Reason is this, every single man, Male and Female, is a perfect Creature of himself; and the same Spirit that made the Globe, dwells in Man to govern the Globe . . . (*A Declaration To The Powers of England and to All the Powers of the World*, 1649.)

Around the same time the Quakers were developing a set of religious beliefs against the use of violence, especially in its ultimate form as war. The quest to establish a democratic and peaceful economy continued as a persistent feature of radical politics during the nineteenth century, expressing itself in different ways in the beliefs of Owenite and Christian socialists, liberal radicals, anarchists, communitarians, and socialists inspired by Morris and Ruskin. This tradition of a radical, democratic socialist pacifism has been incredibly durable as it continued into the twentieth century, taking in new ideas and new forms; thus the influence of Gandhi became important during the 1940s and 1950s, and in the 60s, 70s and 80s, the tradition has been enriched by the views and activities of the environmentalists and the critique of the Greens.

At the same time there has been a tension between those who stand apart from what Mumford called the 'megamachine' of formal politics and industrialism and those, particularly in the labour movement, who work on and within the large structures, but who wish to turn them under popular control to peaceful purposes. The idea of an alternative to the values and structures of violent military industrial systems runs vibrantly through this long tradition and provides a rich quarry in which to search for values, insights and inspiration about the nature of the peaceful economy. Many groups have looked, in a variety of ways, for a means to live their lives according to the values of a nonviolent economy. This diversity should be seen as a strength, a vigorous history of socialist pacifism which has much to say about the nature of a peaceful economy and a peaceful culture. A peaceful economy is unlikely to be found in the possession of any one political ideology, although it is nourished far more in some political traditions than in others.

Throughout the 19th and 20th centuries, the labour movement has been at the forefront of the struggle for democratic rights. The Labour Party, similarly, has done much in providing a wide range of welfare benefits and services which have greatly improved the conditions of the mass of the people. But despite its major achievements, the Labour Party has tended historically to deny the validity of participative economic democracy and co-operation in its preference for bureaucratic and centralised direction. Similarly, few trade unions in modern industrial societies have concerned themselves with the question of fundamentally changing the nature of the relationship between labour and management, or between capital and technology. Trade unionism has been much more concerned to negotiate terms and conditions within the existing framework; at times it has done this remarkably successfully, at other times less so. But by and large there has been built into the mentality and structures of trade unionism an aversion to small-scale production under producers' democracy.

The labour movement for much of the 20th century has

Campaigning in Stevenage by the Direct Action Committee in 1959 led to a strike and demonstration by building workers for diversification of local industry.

defined its political goals in terms of the conquest of power through representation in local and central government, in order to protect the rights of trade unions, and to expand the provision of public services. Ideas concerned with the dynamics of industrial and economic democracy, with common ownership and co-operation, with social control over new technology, and with the special problems of the defence industries have been largely of marginal concern.

Such issues have not, however, been of marginal concern to radical pacifists. During the 1950s and beyond, the Labour Party and the labour movement more broadly was firmly committed to the politics of the mixed economy characterised by a state-managed public sector in tandem with a corporate business enterprise, rationalised, efficient and innovative in technology. An important function of a small number of radicals and pacifists during this period was to keep alive the ideals of the peaceful economy. Wilfred Wellock, for example, was especially important in bringing into the pages of *Peace News* some of the values of Gandhian economics which he had himself encountered and assimilated during the late 1940s.

Wellock, who had been a Labour MP for Stourbridge during the 1930s, visited India during 1949 and became familiar with Gandhian economic values at a conference at Santiniketan. The conference split into a number of commissions, Wellock joining in a group which looked at the relationship between ways of life and work, and the causes of war. On his return to Britain, Wellock published *Gandhi as a Social Revolutionary*, which discussed the importance of Gandhi's ideas in pointing to a third way in economic life, between capitalism on the one hand, and communism on the other. The examples of the Constructive Programme and of Vinoba Bhave's land gift or Bhoodan Movement inspired Wellock, highlighting as they did his own belief in an 'integral pacifism' which implied not only a refusal to countenance violence, but a more positive commitment to a nonviolent way of life. For Wellock it was especially important that one's work, and economic life in general, was based on sound principles.

> . . . war was simply the outward manifestation of inward contradictions within society and within the individual person. Thus the causes of war had to be sought in the way of life and habits of the people.[6]

The idea of trusteeship was crucial to Gandhi's view of

economic relationships, and trusteeship meant that the wealth of the world came from God, and that it was therefore incumbent on those who had become wealthy to share their wealth with the rest of the community. Gandhi's peaceful economy, for those who dislike its foundation in terms of religious justification, has a universal appeal, echoing from the past the values of a long tradition of democratic socialism, and presaging also much of the later values of eco-politics.

> Western economics was based on conflict, and conquest of the earth and human nature. How could such a system survive . . .?
>
> Western economics plundered the earth of irreplaceable resources, and violence against the earth all too easily became violence against people. A nonviolent economy would emphasise not conflict but co-operation, not conquest but harmony with nature. Gandhi called it the 'economy of permanence'. It was held together not simply by necessity and self interest, but by mutual trust and fellowship. (*Peace News* 11 June 1976)

These ideas and values permeated the thinking of a small but influential group of people in Britain in the 1950s, and Wellock, it appears, was the main link between Gandhian politics and British pacifism. During the 1940s he had met Ernest Bader, a Quaker businessman who wished to transform his own company into an enterprise which was closer to true Christian values. Bader in turn was influenced by Wellock, and in 1951 he formed his chemicals company into the Scott Bader Commonwealth. Since then, the company has traded successfully as a medium-sized enterprise manufacturing plastics and polyester resins, and its transformation to common ownership was an explicit attempt to put into practice the ideals of peace and co-operation in one particular business enterprise. The constitution of the Commonwealth in 1951 established six key principles to guide its operation. These were that the firm should not grow beyond a limited size; that there should be a fixed ratio between the highest and lowest paid; that the members of the Commonwealth are partners and not employees; that the Board of Directors should be accountable to the Commonwealth; that the net profits should be divided between the company and the Commonwealth, 60% to the former, and 40% to the latter. Half of the profits appropriated by the Commonwealth were to be paid in bonuses to members, and half to charitable purposes outside the Scott Bader organisation.[7] The final provision was that Scott Bader Ltd should not engage in business known to be concerned with war-related purposes.

Bader and Wellock worked with Harold Farmer, a printer who had also turned his London-based business into a co-operative, to form an organisation to promote the Scott Bader principles more widely. The outcome was Demintry (the Society for Democratic Integration in Industry), which was launched during a public meeting chaired by Wellock and with Bader and Farmer in attendance, in January 1958. In an article in *Peace News*, the treasurer of Demintry, Douglas Stuckey, explained the aims of the new organisation:

> In all its activities Demintry is conscious of the imperative need to decentralise power, to operate in units small enough so that 'all those affected by a decision participate in the making of it'. It seeks to establish organic links between industry and the culture and community in which it works, using modern techniques to effect a Gandhian revolution, giving precedence to men rather than machines. (PN 11 August 1961)

It should be remembered that the Demintry initiative was taken at a time when the number of producers' co-operatives was at an all-time low. The co-operatives which had been formed in the late 19th century influenced by the ideals of Owenism and Christian Socialism and represented by the Co-operative Producers' Federation, were in decline. Growth of the new movement was slow but steady. By 1972, six companies in Britain were said to operate under the principles of the Industrial Common Ownership Movement (ICOM), as Demintry had become in 1971.[8] By the late 1970s, up to 400 co-operatives had registered under the model rules of ICOM, and by 1985 around 1000 co-operatives were trading.

The change from Demintry to ICOM meant a somewhat greater emphasis on the principle of common ownership and control and a less explicit concern with the relationship between militarism and the economy. Even Scott Bader, still trading successfully in 1986, has come under some pressure to undertake research contracts from the Ministry of Defence in order to be able to keep up with the 'state of the art' in their own business. Some staff within the company feel that the original pacifist principles of the Commonwealth may be a hindrance to commercial success and ought to be abandoned. Godric Bader, son of the founder of the company, has resisted these pressures:

> The human species has now developed such prodigious technical

intelligence and skills that it has the power and means not only to cremate itself, but all organic life on planet earth. I simply do not want to play any part or see our Company play any part, in forwarding this macabre technology one whit further if I can avoid doing so . . .. The R + D task in the world that desperately does need our support is how to learn to love and treat our 'enemies' and our neighbours as we would ourselves . . . We do not need the Ministry of Defence but a Ministry of Interdependence to promote international mutual aid and organise a better life for space-ship earth and replace conflict and aggression with co-operation . . . (*Reactor*, Journal of the Scott Bader Community, July 1985)

The dilemma of Scott Bader highlights the central issue for people concerned to develop a peaceful economy, and that is the high consumption of economic resources by the military, and the cost of this to the civil economy.

Arms conversion, the transformation of military production to peaceful purposes, became a frequent theme in *Peace News* from the early 1960s. In 1964, a *Peace News* editorial bemoaned the failure in the White Paper on Defence to even raise the issue of alternatives to spending a projected £2,000 million on defence.

It would not be unreasonable to demand that a sum of — say — £2 million should be devoted to major projects to investigate specific alternatives to the arms race . . . A government which spends a thousand times this sum on defence and refuses to examine the alternatives deserves the strongest possible condemnation. (PN 21 February 1964)

In the absence of such support, pacifists have still struggled to make the connection between militarism, warfare and economic life. The Direct Action Committee (DAC), best known for its dramatic actions at Aldermaston, at the Thor nuclear missile bases in East Anglia and the Midlands, and at the US nuclear submarine base at Holy Loch, also laid the basis for more extensive peacemaking and nonviolent projects. During 1959 the DAC campaigned for two weeks in Stevenage, where the Blue Streak (Britain's intended nuclear missile) was being manufactured. As a consequence, there was a token strike of building trade workers, demanding the diversification of industry in the area. During 1960, campaigns were carried out among trade unions in areas with significant defence industries, at Woodford in the Manchester area, in Bristol, Slough, and Chertsey and Weybridge in Surrey.[9]

In a similar fashion, *Peace News* reported in 1963 the attempt by Tom McAlpine, a member of the Scottish Committee of 100, to set up the Factory for Peace in Glasgow. The Factory for Peace was intended to be an engineering co-operative, with its profits to be split between third world development and the peace movement, while an element was to be ploughed back for its own needs. By May 1964, the co-operative was trading under the name of Rowen Engineering, with 10 full-time workers manufacturing storage heaters. In the following years, a range of articles in *Peace News* covered the problem of the economics of disarmament and ideas related to the conversion of defence industries. In January 1965, to take one example, on the eve of the cancellation of the TSR 2 military aircraft project, the Labour government was strongly condemned for its failure to undertake measures 'for the reconversion to peacetime production of the military economy'. In the absence of a policy for conversion the defence establishment will continue to demand and receive vast resources to maintain and expand the violent economy:

> If there is to be any lesson in all this for the peace movement, it is that the ethics and economics of disarmament must be more aggressively pressed upon the attention of the government and the unions. But ultimately the peace movement will have to face up to the fact that Labour, while willing to reshuffle the military establishment, is no more interested than the Tories in eliminating it. (PN editorial 22 January 1965)

Over twenty years on, very much the same observation could be made. While the Labour Party has moved a long way in its defence policy, and today has an alternative defence strategy, it still has much to do if it is to convince pacifists that it has a real concern to encourage the full development of a peaceful economy. Surely it is time to insist that, in a period when £18 billion annually is spent on defence, there should be some proportionate investment in peace. A Peace Fund (and perhaps such a fund would legitimate and encourage the payment of a peace tax) would do much to sustain a host of important projects which barely survive from year to year. In particular it would make sense, to give one example, to provide funding to the shop stewards in Barrow seeking an alternative to the Trident programme. The Barrow Alternative Employment Committee was given a grant of £12,000 by CND to support a research project into the viability of alternatives to the

In 1976 Lucas Aerospace Workers presented their Alternative Corporate Plan, with 150 suggestions for socially useful products. The bus, which runs either on the road or on rails could extend public transport economically as well as using the skills of workers currently employed in the armaments industry.

Credit: Centre for Alternative Industrial and Technological Systems

production of the Trident submarine. A breakthrough here, where there is so much potential scope for the development of civil marine technology, would be of tremendous practical and symbolic value.[10]

III. The Nonviolent Economy: Contemporary Prospects

Peace is a way of life for persons and nations alike; it emanates from society as scent from roses. (Wilfred Wellock, in *New Horizons*, 1956)

To continue Wellock's analogy of the rose, peace will not just happen. It is a positive state of affairs and must be cultivated. The skills for cultivation are diverse, and different people will find their own preferences and approaches at a variety of levels, whether personal, political, social, economic, or cultural. This article can only suggest some of the guiding principles and practices in recent political and economic activities which might help guide the way towards a peaceful economy.

Profound changes have taken place in the political climate during the 1970s and 1980s. In contrast to the emergence of a resurgent Toryism, the politics of the centre and of the left have lost confidence and faltered during a period of economic recession, technological change, and broader structural changes in the economy. Yet at the same time there has been a renewal of interest in democratic economic planning, both in the labour movement and in the community more generally. The development of new technology and concern about its influence on democracy has called for a fresh assessment of the organisation of work and its relationship to the community.

There has been a change in trade union attitudes towards the role of labour in production, symbolised most of all by the campaign of the Lucas Aerospace Combine Shop Stewards Committee and the wider workers' plans, popular planning, and new technology initiatives which grew up largely under the inspiration of the Lucas model. In case it should be thought that the Lucas Combine initiative failed to achieve all its objectives, it must be remembered that much of practical consequence did result from it in the form of new employment generation programmes in London, and among other local authorities which became concerned about radical responses to inner city decline and unemployment.

Neither should the international reputation of the Lucas Corporate Plan be underestimated. The activities of the

Combine members were followed with interest throughout the world. Indeed the Combine was nominated for the Nobel Peace Prize, and failing to win it, was awarded instead the peace prize of the Right Livelihood Foundation, the so-called alternative Nobel prize.

During the 1970s there has also been a revival of workers' co-operation, along with an admittedly cautious acceptance within the labour movement that co-operatives should have a more central role to play in the political and economic strategies of labour. Radical and democratic employment strategies have been initiated by a number of local authorities, and *Peace News* has covered many of these developments in recent years. At the local and regional levels, a great deal of energy is being devoted to the cultivation of new forms of democratic enterprise. Such initiatives raise the possibility of the eventual emergence of a new economic order, which is dependent neither on the free market, nor the central state, but which tends towards associations of producers in localities or regions, eventually growing to form a federation of self-managed enterprises.[11]

Frequently, in *Peace News*, the crisis of unemployment has been interpreted in an important sense as having a positive feature, presenting the opportunity to construct something new out of the ruins of the old industrial culture. Guy Dauncey, for example, has written about the beginning of a community economics, a diversity of locally based enterprise which will eventually amount to a new local economic order:

> the groundwork is clear for a new local economic order: a homemade equivalent perhaps of the new international economic order. At present, we are just seeing one-off initiatives, scattered here and there, existing within the financial structures of mainstream capitalism. (PN 5 March 1982)

Similarly, James Robertson, in 'What Comes After Full Employment?', *The Other Economic Summit* (1984), has written of the failure of conventional industrialism and the opportunity offered by a positive and democratic vision of a post-industrial future. Three future scenarios are envisioned. On the one hand, a business as usual approach which assumes the continuation of the existing dominant economic powers and relationships, where continued expansion in the industrialised world will provide markets for Third World products. Secondly, a hyperexpansionist, or HE, vision of a post-industrial future where the majority live lives of leisure in a world automated and largely free of labour, administered and controlled by a highly skilled technocratic elite. The best hope for the future, however, lies in Robertson's third scenario, which he calls sane, humane, and ecological, or SHE — an economy which is locally based on a diversity of skills and on mutual aid, and where new technology developments will enhance local economic autonomy. Advanced small-scale technologies have the capacity to bring productive work back into the home, the neighbourhood, and the locality, and the outcome will be an 'ownwork society'.

It is good and important to have such optimistic visions, but necessary also to point to their limitations and to obstacles to their realisations. One problem is highlighted by the frequent objection that the stress on local democratic economies is over-optimistic and misrepresents what is really happening in the world at large and in the main centres of political and economic power. As Brian Davey, in a criticism of Dauncey's approach, commented:

> . . . things are going in just the opposite direction . . . The growth in the power of the national and multinational companies surely overrides by far the development of co-ops and community ventures. The latter, to be sure, are on the increase. They are valuable as an example of the way in which workers (and communities) can control economic enterprises, but they are still microscopic in terms of numbers of jobs when compared with unemployment, let alone the mainstream economy . . . (PN 14 May 1982)

Such objections point to the need for greater structural support which would encourage the vigorous growth of local economic democracy and improve understanding of the relationship between the local economy and the national, multinational, and global economies. Again, *Peace News* has provided a forum for clarifying and debating these issues, and the proceedings of The Other Economic Summit (TOES) have advanced and analysed a number of policies (financial, economic, and political) to assist the practical problems facing people pioneering democratic economic enterprise.

Dauncey has recognised the need to nourish the local economy, while designing a means for it to co-exist with a peaceful global economy. This means that the question of political policy and control must be recognised and acted upon. In 'The New Local Economic Order', his contribution to *The*

Other Economic Summit (1984), Dauncey suggests that the local political authority should recognise and enforce three 'Codes of Conduct' to which all enterprises in the local economy would have to adhere. Firstly, the Right Livelihood Code, which would guarantee democratic and flexible working patterns. Secondly, a Right Relationship With Nature Code, which would force enterprises to abandon polluting manufacturing practices, and positively discriminate, with financial incentives in favour of practices which were ecologically sound and which tended to promote a self-reliant energy policy. Thirdly, a Right Relationship With The Planet Code, which would guide the relationship between local and global investment and economic activity generally. One specific measure would be for a local economy to twin with an equivalent community in the southern hemisphere or Third World, and to channel funds to that economy by means of small 'trickle up' grants to help initiate and develop enterprises.

Similar principles, although related to the responsibilities of the state, were suggested by Andre Gorz in his *Farewell To The Working Class: An Essay on Post Industrial Socialism* (Pluto Press, 1980). Gorz has argued strongly that a peaceful economic and post-industrial future cannot entail simply the return to traditional crafts and the village economy. He has identified two spheres of work activity; one he calls heteronomous work, which does depend on the standardisation of production, the division of labour, and the mass production of goods by machines. The second sphere of work is autonomous activity, where people have an increased right of access to convivial tools. Convivial tools are tools which allow creative labour based on voluntary co-operation or personal activity. However, it is impossible to have free creative autonomous activity without some element of heteronomous activity, because

> it is impossible to imagine that telephones, video machines, microprocessors, bicycles or photoelectric cells — all potentially convivial tools that can be put to autonomous purposes — could be produced at the level of a family, a group, or a local community.

What is important is that the sphere of autonomy should be enlarged for all, and that correspondingly, the less rewarding socialised mass-production should be minimised and shared. Gorz described his utopia as a possible dual society which would operate under basic principles; three in particular were important. Firstly, that people should work less, and that they should be able to satisfy their needs whether or not they had a job. Secondly, products should be designed and produced in order to provide the greatest satisfaction both to those who made and to those who used them. Design criteria would be based on durability, ease of repair, pleasantness of manufacture, and absence of polluting effects. Thirdly, it was necessary to recover and extend individual and social autonomy, to re-integrate culture into daily life, and to spread skills and arts and the means to acquire them. In these ways the dictatorship of the state, by over-reliance on it, would be avoided.

Gorz emphasises central political regulation and socialised ownership and control of the large enterprises in a way that might concern and alarm pacifists and others from a more libertarian tradition. Still, there is considerable evidence that the principles of smallness of scale, of ecological responsibility, and of decentralised control have entered neo-marxist modes of thinking. Some people will prefer to 'act local' and avoid mass politics; others may see the big institutions of labour, capital, technology, and political authorities as the significant focal points on which to concentrate in the endeavour to continue to cultivate peaceful economics.

The entrenchment and expansion of arms production as a leading characteristic of industrial economies is the economic feature which most of all threatens peace. One theme, consequently, which deserves over-riding consideration in the design of the peaceful economy is the importance of turning back the proliferating tide of weapons production and export which characterises the violent economic relationships of the industrial nations, and of those countries throughout the world which attempt to emulate them. To Dauncey's three codes of conduct mentioned above, we should therefore add one which positively supports initiatives for peaceful production . . . a Technology for Peace Code.

The conversion of defence industries to production for peaceful purposes has long been advocated within the radical and pacifist traditions, and has been consistently covered within the pages of *Peace News*. Defence conversion is often seen to be only a means of dealing with excess capacity in the defence industries, a means of cutting them back to suit the evolving patterns of weapons design, and to find alternative work for displaced arms workers. But peace conversion implies a broader and more imaginative vision, pointing to the need to dismantle economic conflict formations which lead to war, and to replace them with a democratic and peaceful technology. The conversion approach towards disarmament stresses the potential common interests between peace and labour groups in diverting resources from military to civilian or social use.

Too often this objective is justified purely in terms of reviving the national economy, while neglecting questions concerning global development. For a number of years, the relationship between disarmament and development has been a priority of the United Nations, yet a series of promising proposals have been shelved because of the inertia of governments, and the absence of peace movements capable of acting internationally. Yet there have been hopeful developments in recent years. Alternative disarmament strategies are being advanced in Europe and the USA, capable not only of protesting against nuclear weapons, but of posing new defence options based on ideas of defensive deterrence. These developments need to be enhanced by the promotion of international contacts and networks capable of fusing locally, regionally, and nationally based projects with transnational disarmament and development goals.[12] It is a good sign that this process is beginning to occur. To give one example, in 1984 an International Economic Conversion Conference was held in Boston and discussed an agenda for action which included the proposal to begin a dialogue between workers in the OECD and non-industrial countries on the direction of global industrialism. This dialogue could take place within the context of a strengthening of ties between international conversion advocates, and the creation of an international conversion campaign.

> Peace, as has often been said, is indivisible — how then could peace be built on a foundation of reckless science and violent technology? (*Small is Beautiful*, p. 27)

Schumacher's question poses in a nutshell the importance of taking care of the economic dimension of peace. But it is heartening to conclude that despite the visibility of the large and violent systems, tangible in weapons and wasteful technologies, there is still a flourishing sector of local skills and small-scale democratic enterprise, and a desire to sustain and develop the economy of peace.

1. A J Pierre, *The Global Politics of Arms Sales*, Princeton University Press, 1982.

2. Wilfred Wellock, *New Horizons*, 1956.

3. Seymour Melman, *The Permanent War Economy* 1972 See also D Smith and R Smith, *The Economics of Militarism*, Pluto Press, London, 1983.

4. The figures on which table 1 is based were taken from 'Royal Ordnance: Moving Into the Front Line', *Grievson Grant Investment Research*, 1984.

5. See, for example, Lewis Mumford, *The Myth of the Machine: Technics and Human Development*, Secker and Warburg, London 1966.

6. Wilfred Wellock, 'The Khadi World', July 1952. I am grateful to Andrew Rigby for the opportunity to read his biography of Wellock while it was in draft form. This quote is taken from Rigby's forthcoming biography of Wellock.

7. E F Schumacher, 'The Scott Bader Commonwealth', *Sarvodaya*, xxii, no. 2, Sept., 1972.

8. These companies were Scott Bader Commonwealth; Landsman Co-ownership Ltd; Rowen Engineering (South Wales and Glasgow, also known as the Factories for Peace); Trylon Ltd; and Michael Jones Jewellers Ltd.

9. I have relied on Michael Randle's 'The Strategy of Nonviolent Direct Action' for this account. This is a draft article, to be published shortly.

10. The report by their research worker, Steve Schoofield, will be published in June 1986 by the School of Peace Studies at Bradford University.

11. This possibility is put forward as a potential outcome of Lucas type initiatives in H Wainwright and D Elliott, *The Lucas Plan*, Alison and Busby, London, 1982. An account of the new worker co-operatives, including Triumph Meriden and the Scottish Daily News, is given in K Coates (ed.), *The New Worker Co-operatives*, Spokesman Books, Nottingham, 1976.

12. Unfortunately there is not the space here to cover recent work on defence industries and defence conversion. Those wanting to know more might look at *Peace Research Reports* numbers 6, 7 and 8 published by the School of Peace Studies, University of Bradford; these cover developments in the USA and the UK.

Be Practical, Do the Impossible: The Politics of Everyday Life

Andrew Rigby

In November 1918, the state government of Bavaria was overthrown by a force of soldiers and workers who proclaimed the establishment of the Bavarian Democratic and Social Republic. Barely seven months later, the short-lived socialist republic was crushed by an army of 100,000. Amongst the 700 who were killed was the anarcho-pacifist Gustav Landauer. Some years later, in 1925, a monument was erected to his memory in Munich by the Anarchist-Syndicalist Union. It bore an inscription from Landauer:

> Now is the time to bring forth a martyr of a different kind, not heroic, but a quiet unpretentious martyr who will provide an example for the proper life.

For Landauer, the state and capitalism could not be attacked directly by means of the ballot box or the bomb. The roots of such oppressive institutions lay in the human spirit, in habits of dependence, routine and inertia — and the consequent belief in the need for leadership that made possible the persistence of such alien bodies as the state. According to Landauer:

> The state is a condition, a certain relationship between human beings, a mode of human behaviour; we destroy it by contracting other relationships, by behaving differently.

In other words, so long as we confront each other as separate individuals, we make the coercive state necessary. To the extent that we come together and fashion new, non-coercive relationships, attempting to counter our own 'inner statehood', we begin to render the state unnecessary and superfluous. From this point of view, we are always helping to undermine and destroy systems of oppression to the extent that we enter into new relationships of mutual aid and co-operation. For Landauer,

Anarchy is not a thing of the future, but of the present; not a matter of demands but of living.[1]

According to this perspective, the real revolutionary project entails the construction of a socialist reality in the here-and-now rather than waiting for the day of THE Revolution. The true revolutionary process takes place through education in self-reliance and mutual aid, and in co-operative organisations that can become the organs of a new society. The struggle for social transformation can only bear fruit when, in Landauer's words, 'we are seized by the spirit, not of revolution, but of regeneration'.[2]

This emphasis on the crucial significance of reconstructing individual and collective life in the process of liberation was also central to Gandhi's thought and action. True swaraj, or independence, could only be achieved on the basis of self-reliant individuals who co-operated together to create 'village republics' as the cells of a new social order informed by the values of mutual aid, self-sufficiency, non-exploitation and nonviolence.

Within the Western pacifist tradition the emphasis on the essential continuity between the processes of individual and social change, the conviction that 'the personal is political', is perhaps most closely associated with the names of Thoreau and Tolstoy. Writing in 1849 in his essay 'On the Duty of Civil Disobedience', Thoreau affirmed the moral duty of the enlightened individual to struggle against the injustices of society and the state in accord with the dictates of their conscience: 'The only obligation I have a right to assume is to do at any time what I think right' — even if this meant letting one's life become a 'counter-friction' against the machinery of government. For Tolstoy, likewise, the greatest force at hand for the transformation of the social order was the refusal of individuals to co-operate with the state and obey its immoral demands. For both of them it was more important to be a good neighbour than a good citizen. Individuals have a duty to observe a higher moral code than that of the state, the purpose of life being to exemplify goodness and abstain from participating in any form of violence.

In the development of his ideas Tolstoy was influenced by the example of such world-rejecting anabaptist groups as the Doukhobours and the Hutterites, who could trace back to the 16th century their attempts to pursue a divinely ordained way of life by means of communities of believers, withdrawn from the profane world. In Britain a fairly continuous thread of attempts to establish alternative ways of life, microcosms of a new social order, can be traced back at least to the 17th century when Gerard Winstanley and the Diggers tried to establish a 'Heaven on Earth' in Surrey, on through various religious and secular groups, up to the utopian socialist experiments of Robert Owen and others in the 19th century.

In point of fact, Tolstoy disapproved of attempts to establish what he depicted as 'communities of saints among sinners', but this did not prevent the growth of a 'Tolstoyan movement' in Russia, Europe and North America by the end of the last century. In Britain, as elsewhere, people who had been influenced by his political, social and religious ideas attempted to form co-operative colonies or communities where they sought to lead simple lives of ethical purity, untainted by the evils of capitalism and, in the process, provide practical demonstrations of the relevance of such ventures to the dilemmas of mainstream society. Thus, in May 1894, John Coleman Kenworthy established the Brotherhood Church in Croydon and in 1896 a group of men and women from the church formed a Tolstoyan community at Purleigh.[3] A year later, a related experiment was launched in Leeds, with the establishment of the Brotherhood Workshop. In 1898, the Whiteway Colony was formed on Tolstoyan lines in Gloucester-shire, whilst early in the following year an offshoot of the Leeds community was founded at Blackburn. Tom Ferris, one of the members of the Blackburn community, explained how, recognising no authority beyond the dictates of their own conscience they were determined to live their lives according to the teachings of Jesus as laid out in the Sermon on the Mount. They came to believe,

> that love is the denial of force, even of resistance to evil by any force or compulsion; that truth involves perfect openness and sincerity in all our dealings; and that spiritual life is only co-existent with entire purity; that these principles when carried out will bring about peace on earth and good will and brotherly love to mankind.[4]

In their resistance to any compromise between their conception of the ways of God and the ways of the world, the members of such Tolstoyan pacifist communities were particularly strict in their rejection of any compromise between professed belief and actual practice. As such, they remained a minority within the broader movement for social change at the turn of the century, whilst simultaneously constituting an integral component of that wider movement. There was a strong revivalist fervour about much of the socialist propagandising of the 1880s and 1890s, nourished in part by the non-conformist vision of a Christian commonwealth. It was a period when socialism was considered to be much more a moral crusade for a new way of life than a party-political struggle for state power. There was a firm conviction that social structural change was indivisible from personal change, that socialism was attainable, if only sufficient numbers of people could be fired with the appropriate virtues. The writings of people such as William Morris, Edward Carpenter, Ruskin and Kropotkin were discussed in clubs, meeting rooms, debating societies, Socialist Sunday Schools, and mutual improvement classes throughout the country. Morris's *News From Nowhere* was perhaps the fullest expression of the themes that permeated such discussions. In it, he portrayed a decentralised society of largely self-governing communities wherein the dignity and creativity of human labour had been reclaimed through the reduction of large-scale industry and the reintegration of town and country, urban and rural production. For Morris, the principle task was to 'make socialists', and the progress of the movement was to be judged by the capacity of such socialists to exemplify in their daily lives those values and practices which would characterise the hoped-for society of the future.

According to Wilfred Wellock, it was the depression years of the late 1920s and 1930s that killed off what remained of this idealistic, ethical socialism. He maintained that,

> It was in the 'thirties' that the 'bread and butter politics' of the new materialism completely overwhelmed the spiritual idealism of the earlier Socialists. The decline of that idealism was quickly followed by the rapid spread of the materialistic values of capitalism among the working classes, including the Trade Unions and the Labour Party. This meant that henceforth Party politics would degenerate into a power struggle for the right to determine which social classes or groups should benefit most from the financial policies of the Government.[5]

Indeed, by the outbreak of the Second World War only a few of the original experiments in communal living remained in existence — albeit in modified form. These included the Whiteway Colony, and the Brotherhood Church at Stapleton in

Yorkshire. There was also the Cotswold Bruderhof of the Society of Brothers that had been founded by Eberhard Arnold in Germany in the inter-war years, whose members had moved to Britain to avoid Nazi persecution. During 1940–41 they moved on again, this time to Paraguay, leaving a small number behind as the nucleus of a new community — the Wheathill Bruderhof in Shropshire.

However, the tradition refused to die, and within two years of the outbreak of war, agriculturally-based pacifist centres of alternative living were springing up all over the country. By the spring of 1940, the Germans had achieved their military breakthrough in Europe, the period of the 'phoney war' was over, and pacifist appeals for a negotiated peace seemed increasingly irrelevant. It appeared as if the world was sinking deeper and deeper into the pit of barbarism. Pacifists had no immediately practical political solutions to offer, and so it seemed to some that there was a need to redirect the pacifist project towards a longer time-scale. If the immediate future offered little but the extension of totalitarianism around the globe, perhaps the only valid role for pacifists was to revert to their traditional status as a redemptive minority — a small band of prophetic witnesses to an alternative set of values and way of life that might some day save the world from destruction. As early as 1935, one of the key movers behind this re-orientation, Max Plowman, had written that the problem facing pacifists was not so much how to stop war but rather 'how to live like a human individual in order that you might live socially and communally'.[6] His close friend, John Middleton Murry, who replaced Humphrey Moore as editor of *Peace News* in July 1940, had come to a similar conclusion by 1938, when he suggested that 'the real business of a pacifist movement is to bear its witness against the total dehumanisation of humanity that is necessitated by modern war . . .'.[7] Wilfred Wellock, who was appointed 'Honorary Consulting Editor' of *Peace News* along-side Murry, came to endorse this position, arguing that the key role of the pacifist was 'to envisage the future and to seek ways and means of saving and introducing those values without which human existence ceases to have any meaning'. (*Peace News*, June 14, 1940) For Wellock the fulfilment of this prophetic role required the adoption of an 'integrated pacifism', a 'politics of creative living'. As the origins of war lay in our whole way of life and the materialistic values upon which it was based, it was necessary to transform society from the bottom upwards, starting with our own lives. Wars would cease not when people refused to fight, but only when people had learnt how to live.

Nearly 1000 acres of farmland was purchased in Lincolnshire during 1941 for the purpose of training pacifists who wished to join agricultural colonies. Eventually over 50 community projects were established. They included not only land-based colonies, but also urban income-sharing groups. Conferences were held, books published and, in March 1941, *Peace News* began publishing a monthly supplement devoted to the coverage of community projects and the ideas behind them. Unfortunately, the lived experience of those seeking to establish the seed-beds of a qualitatively new civilisation was to prove rather more problematic than the theory had led them to anticipate.

Ronald Duncan described his experience in a community he established in North Devon. This revealed to him 'the depths of stupid childishness to which so many moderately intelligent people are brought when they are involved in any sort of communal activity'.[8] He came to realise that many of those who professed their commitment to exploring a new alternative way of life carried with them quite a few of the faults of the old civilisation upon which they had turned their backs. Middleton Murry, who had bought a 182 acre farm in 1942, in order to establish a community, came to share this opinion. Idealistic young pacifists who tended to repudiate any externally imposed discipline on ideological grounds, who devalued notions of tidiness and punctuality as 'bourgeois', who were convinced that good manners were a sign of self-repression, and who were prepared to discuss such matters at all hours rather than get on with the routine chores of farming — this was not the most suitable human resource with which to construct the embryo of a new age. Like communities before and since, Murry's venture seemed to attract more than its share of eccentrics and oddballs:

> When I look back over those trying years, I seem to see a procession of social misfits entering and departing from the farm. We found it hard to resist an appeal to our charity. From the nature of our efforts we felt obliged to maintain a higher standard of generosity than the outside world . . . to give at least temporary shelter and a trial to people whom a strictly practical enterprise would never have considered.[9]

As in so many utopian communities, the idealism of the truly committed made them easy prey for the parasitism of those seeking a refuge from the demands of conventional existence. Murry went on:

> Young pacifists are suspect. Unless by their works they definitely prove the contrary, it may be assumed that the majority of them are seeking to escape social responsibility, though they may be unconscious of it. They made poor material for a long term effort. Half of them, as soon as the war was over, went back eagerly to their pre-war jobs: the vocation for co-operative agriculture which they had professed was merely an alibi.

Dennis Hayes was more charitable in his admission that 'the best thinkers (and talkers) were not always the best workers . . . The pattern of community life imposed a strain that many were untrained to bear: the fundamental need was for self-discipline, and though the "communiteers" had often seen the Promised Land from afar, their provision for the journey was often sketchy in the extreme'.[10]

For Wilfred Wellock, the collapse of so many of the pacifist communities by the end of the war constituted one of the major disappointments of his life. However, he continued to advocate and practise a simple, non-acquisitive life-style: emphasising the themes of self-reliance, voluntary poverty, organic horti-culture, bread labour; urging people to develop the art of 'localising, nationalising, and internationalising neighbour-liness'. Writing in 1947, Aldous Huxley maintained that Wellock was one of the few isolated voices seeking to restate the old doctrine of self-reliance and mutual aid within a localised co-operative community. In the midst of 'the enormous bellowing chorus of advertisers singing the praises of centralised mass-producing and mass-distributing industry, and of left-wing propagandists singing the praise of the omnipotent state', people like Wellock in Britain and Ralph Borsodi in the United States constituted a 'tiny piece of decentralist leaven' within 'the whole large lump of contemporary society'.[11] In fact, by the time of his death in 1972, Wellock could derive some satisfaction from the fact that the emphasis on pacifism as an integral way of life had begun to encroach in again from the margins of the wider peace movement, in the guise of what became known variously as the counter-culture and the alternative society.

One of the chief ideologues of this movement was the one-time editor of *Peace News*, Theodor Roszak, who sought to locate the new counter-cultural movement for an alternative society within the utopian tradition of anarcho-pacifism, its project being nothing less than the proclamation of a new heaven and a new earth.[12] *Peace News* was a key medium for this emergent movement, with its emphasis on creating alternative institutions, transforming individual consciousness, and establishing non-exploitative interpersonal relationships in the here-and-now as a means of transforming the wider society. The notion of self-change for social change became a recurring theme in the paper. By the early 1970s a considerable amount of space was being devoted to the coverage of alternative projects such as free schools, free universities, communes, food co-operatives, alternative economics and workers' co-operatives, alternative technology and energy sources, and alternative psychiatry. Readers were enjoined to examine the totality of their lifestyle and restructure it in the direction of liberation of the self and the establishment of non-coercive relationships with others and nature.

In the harsher economic climate of recent years, it has become almost fashionable within radical circles to dismiss the alternative society movement of the late 1960s and 1970s as little more than the empty symbolic posturing of disaffected but affluent middle class youth. Indeed, in retrospect, a lot of the criticisms appear valid. In the emphasis upon transforming lifestyles there was, perhaps, too much emphasis placed on *style*. At least part of the movement was more concerned with fashion than a serious attempt to restructure the patterns of domination in society. It seemed to some that there was an over-emphasis on purely individualistic solutions to the angst of contemporary existence, and thereby a devaluation of economic and material issues which meant that the alternative movement struck few chords within the hearts and minds of most 'ordinary folk'. To many people it appeared that the challenging of the work ethic, which was an integral part of the counter-culture, was little more than a celebration of idleness by the privileged off-spring of the middle class, who could afford to escape from the exigencies of 'having to earn a living' into their arcadian communes, where they could sit around experimenting with their consciousness by ingesting a variety of organic and inorganic substances. Although this is something of a caricature there is substance to the image. There was a strong element of cultural elitism about much of the counter-culture that involved a dismissal of the

From 1970 some thousand squatters created the Free Town of Christiana in a 54-acre disused barracks in Copenhagen. Credit: Suzanne Mertz

mundane concerns of 'straights'. Too often the 'advance posts of the alternative society' became cultural ghettos where the traditional pacifist emphasis on the means of change rather than the ends was devalued into a narcissistic focusing on the 'self'. Moreover, the elevation of individual freedom to an absolute value often led to a facile emphasis on 'doing your own thing' which, in practice, meant being a victim to every passing whim and a diminution of respect for the rights of others. The idealistic emphasis on consciousness as the critical variable too often degenerated into an apparent assumption that oppression and domination could be overcome simply and solely by thinking differently.

And yet, despite all these negative attributes, the movement for an alternative society cannot be dismissed as a cultural aberration. Alongside all the weaknesses that one associates with the utopian/anarcho-pacifist tradition, there were corresponding strengths. The movement was characterised by an enormous creativity that came from the utopian confidence that nothing is impossible. The widening and deepening of the conception of struggle beyond a narrow concern with class embraced domination and oppression in all areas of life. Moreover, the emphasis on the importance of embodying the future in the present means of struggle (especially the concern with developing non-hierarchical forms of organising) has become central to a variety of contemporary social movements, especially the women's movement.

In part, the women's movement emerged in reaction to the perceived gap between the rhetoric and the practice of the counter-culture and related liberation movements of the later 1960s and early 1970s. Indeed, from one point of view, it is possible to argue that women's liberation took off where the alternative movement stopped — it shared the call for a re-evaluation of the social roles into which the sexual division of labour casts men and women, but it insisted that this restructuring extended beyond the confines of the sub-cultural niches of the communes and other alternative institutions into the realm of mainstream life. The slogan 'the personal is political' took on a far broader and deeper significance under the promptings of the women's liberation movement. Moreover, in its emphasis on patriarchy as the defining characteristic underpinning domination in all its many guises, feminism extended the analysis that had informed many of the more thoughtful and perceptive advocates of the alternative society. Indeed, the 'Alternative Socialism' group which was closely associated with *Peace News* made a serious attempt to develop the insights of the alternative society in a manner which would make them relevant to 'ordinary people' and, as part of that, the wider labour movement. For at least some of the members of this libertarian socialist group, patriarchy was a central plank of their analysis as they argued that 'prick power is no basis for socialism'.[13]

Other people around *Peace News* pursued a similar project of making the concerns of the counter-culture more relevant to other areas of oppression. In a pamphlet published in 1978, *Taking Racism Personally*, they wrote:

> We are writing as members of a movement for nonviolent revolution and alternatives. We are painfully aware that as a movement we have slept on the issue of racism . . . We know . . . that any serious anti-racist work must educate itself to the everyday realities of institutional racism through dialogue with Black people and in practical struggle against these racist institutions. But perhaps . . . before pushing into 'Action' we should become more aware of our own racism, the racism of our own traditions — liberal and left wing included.[14]

The focus was still on the individual and the 'politics of everyday life', but it did constitute a serious attempt to link this 'alternative' approach to a struggle to transform the structures of oppression and domination in society.

The point I am trying to make is that beyond the caricature image of the alternative society — 'brown rice and sandals', 'peace and jam' and all the rest — there was a significant attempt to reclaim the utopian tradition of anarcho-pacifism and make it relevant to the issues of the last quarter of the 20th century. In doing this, the movement has reaffirmed the essential continuity between personal and social change, between revolutionary means and ends. In the process it has kept alive the positive vision of a nonviolent society and way of life for which we must strive. Such a vision, and such a hope, is essential in the present age if we are to avoid sinking into despair at the prospect of the imminent threat of nuclear destruction, the continuing rape of nature, and the growing obscenity of gross inequality in all its many manifestations.

'But we seem as far from the co-operative commonwealth as ever!' observes the realist. However, for the utopian there are some positive signs. The advocates of a simpler, more self-reliant, integrated, morally responsible, ecologically sound and co-operative way of life have traditionally been dismissed as cranks. But, as we look around the contemporary scene, it is possible to discern a growing interest in the kinds of ideas and practices that have informed the utopian proponents of an alternative social order. Decentralisation, 'small is beautiful', the limitation of material wants, co-operative production, — all these ideas and more have started to encroach in from the 'cranky' margins.

But are they encroaching fast enough to avert the threat of destruction that is so imminent? 'Surely,' the political realist might argue, 'however beautiful the vision, however pure the means, the urgency of the present situation requires immediate practical and relevant action?' Indeed, the awareness of the immediate crisis has led many radicals who have hitherto eschewed parliamentary politics into the 'real-politik' of state politics. Many proponents of the alternative society have joined the Labour Party in Britain in recent years, acknowledging its manifold faults but driven by a sense of urgency to achieve something 'before it is too late'. After all, they reason, there are some grounds for believing that a Labour Government might make significant steps towards nuclear disarmament alongside a more caring and socially responsible set of policies in the domestic sphere. It would all fall far short of the vision of a co-operative commonwealth, a libertarian society of voluntary associations and small societies, but surely it would be a step on the way?

It is a difficult dilemma — how should we act to change (and save) the world? In addressing this problem, the German sociologist, Max Weber, distinguished between two ideal types of ethical systems in the sphere of politics. Firstly, there is the ethic of ultimate ends (or conviction), characterised by an uncompromising commitment to a set of values and ideals, and there is the ethic of responsibility, which acknowledges a need to be guided in one's political conduct by a sense of what is realistically possible within the parameters of existing conditions. The latter accepts the need for compromise with the realities of the world-as-it-is, recognises the necessity for pragmatism, bargaining and choosing between lesser evils if one is to operate effectively in the profane world of politics.

It was Weber's pessimistic conclusion that neither of these

two modes could act as infallible guides to action. Thus, with regard to the ethics of conviction: either it can lead to the belief that the good end justifies morally dubious means, a path that can lead to the Gulag; or it can lead to the rejection of all but the purest of means, with a consequent failure to resist immediate evils in any effective manner. The pathway directed by the ethic of responsibility also has its dangers and its pitfalls. You compromise once, a second time, and before you know it, the dream has been lost in a morass of technical problems involved in making the present system work. Think of the rich vision of the early socialists and compare it with the poverty of the contemporary Labour Party, a devaluing of the socialist project that has accompanied the elevation of the pursuit of parliamentary power above all else. Sometimes it seems to me that the main reason advanced for supporting the Labour Party is to 'kick the Tories out' — truly a choice between two evils!

The problem remains. Is there a way of reconciling the two modes of political conduct, a way of combining conviction with responsibility, a way of maintaining the vision of the ideal whilst acknowledging the world-as-it-is? Is there a way of resolving the paradox of consequences: that the best of intentions can lead to disastrous results? Is the notion of a 'practical utopianism' a total absurdity?

In 1968, the radical students of France urged us to 'Be realistic, demand the impossible'. In equipping ourselves to attempt the impossible, we could do worse than draw upon the insights and themes that have been the hallmark of the alternative tradition over generations. If we are to have a future, we need to see the whole of our daily life as an arena of struggle. The quest for a new social order needs to focus not just on the workplace but on the community, not just on the relationship between classes but on the relationships within classrooms, not just on the material conditions of life but on the spiritual condition of the individual psyche.

But what about being practical, being responsible? Being responsible surely implies acting with due regard for the consequences of our conduct. It involves recognising the extent to which we contribute to the exploitation of people, animals and nature, in our everyday lives. It involves acknowledging, with Gandhi, that 'all exploitation is based on co-operation, willing or forced, of the exploited . . . there would be no exploitation if people refused to obey the exploiters'. It is this

The peace camps of the 1980s continue the tradition of nonviolence both as resistance and immediate personal change. One of the women's peace camps at Greenham Common, July 1985.

Credit: Bob Naylor

insight which is at the heart of 'direct action' — the expression of our claim to be autonomous, responsible, caring citizens of our society.

The peace camps can be viewed as the most significant recent manifestation of this tradition. One member of the Greenham Common women's peace camp depicted the camp as an experiment in nonviolent resistance which involved 'the taking of responsibility by ordinary people, not just for what's being done in our name, but for how we behave towards each other'.[15] As with previous attempts to challenge the existing order through the creation of alternative structures, attempts have been made to devalue the witness of the peace campers by depicting them as a marginal minority. However, like the members of previous minorities within the alternative tradition, their impact on others who 'take the message home' and work for change in their own communities should not be under-estimated. The peace camps continue to remind us that 'direct action' is not something to be confined to occasional demonstrations. Rather, it requires us to practise and exercise our capacity for self-management and mutual aid in all areas of life.

We can all begin to make gradual changes in the way we live, evolving one step at a time towards a truly nonviolent lifestyle, facing our own challenges in our own way and at our own pace. For some, this might lead to an involvement in the world of party politics, for others it can lead to attempts at self-sufficient communal living. What is crucial to whichever path is pursued is the preparedness to engage in a constant process of conscious evaluation of the relationship between our values and visions, our lifestyles and our 'public' action. Only by seeking to maintain some essential continuity between means and ends can we remain faithful to the truth that generations of utopians have sought to embody: an organic nonviolent social order can only grow from the seeds that we sow in our everyday lives and actions. Only by seeking to transform ourselves at the same time as we strive to reconstruct our institutions can we hope to achieve the impossible, and thereby avert the unthinkable.

And finally — we could do worse than bear in mind the first stanza of D H Lawrence's 'A Sane Revolution':

If you make a revolution, make it for fun,
don't make it in ghastly seriousness,
don't do it in deadly earnest,
do it for fun.

1. Quoted in E Lunn, *Prophet of Community*, Berkeley: University of California Press, 1973, p 35.

2. Quoted in C W, 'Gustav Landauer', *Anarchy*, 54, August 1965, p 247.

3. See M J De K Holman, 'The Purleigh Colony: Tolstoyan Togetherness in the late 1890s', in M Jones, ed, *New Essays on Tolstoy*, Cambridge: Cambridge University Press, 1978.

4. Quoted in A G Higgins, *A History of the Brotherhood Church*, Stapleton: Brotherhood Church, 1982, p 18.

5. W Wellock, *Off the Beaten Track*, Tanjore: Sarvodaya Prachuralaya, 1961, p 65.

6. Letter to Jack Common, in D L P, ed, *Bridge into the Future*, London: Andrew Dakers, 1944, p 547.

7. J Middleton Murry, *The Pledge of Peace*, London: PPU, 1938, p 10.

8. R Duncan, *All Men Are Islands*, London: Hart Davis, 1964, p 230.

9. J Middleton Murry, *Community Farm*, London: Peter Nevill, 1952, p 98.

10. D Hayes, *Challenge of Conscience*, London: Allen and Unwin, 1949, p 217.

11. A Huxley, *Science, Liberty and Peace*, London: Chatto and Windus, 1947, p 43.

12. See T Roszak, *The Making of a Counter Culture*, London: Faber & Faber, 1970.

13. See Keith Paton, *Alternative Socialism*, Birmingham: Birmingham Alternative Socialism Group, 1976, p 22.

14. *Taking Racism Personally*, Nottingham: Peace News, 1978, p 1.

15. Quoted in A Cook & G Kirk, *Greenham Women Everywhere*, London: Pluto, 1983, p 29.

Shelter From the Storm: Under the Green Umbrella

by Chris Jones

'People should take control of their own lives' is something I've heard Tony Benn emphasise. Liberals and even conservatives could find something in it. It says 'people' as a collective, but the 'own' reflects something personal. *Peace News* says it every fortnight. We may all have different interpretations of a society built around these simple words, but the common slogan indicates the appeal of the essentially anarchist idea. The appeal is widespread, even more so today, when so many bad decisions affecting our own lives are taken by remote people in large and impersonal institutions.

In asserting control over their own lives, a number of social groups have been galvanised into new social movements that are presenting a *political* challenge, whilst a crisis in political representation reigns within the existing parliamentary institutions and parties. I haven't the space to go into why this crisis has arisen, but will point to three extremely significant facts: the new social movements have appeared roughly *at the same time*; they have arisen *outside* of the established political process; and they have arrived, to varying degrees, in *all* the Western democracies.

The form of the new social movements is important, as important as the content of their message. It is this similarity of form that serves as a basis to unite the movements and will lay the foundations for a more politically pluralistic society in the future. This form is shaped by some of the guiding principles that inform the ecological movement, which I will discuss later in this essay.

The new social movements are grouped around two political areas — *liberation*-based politics and *issue*-based politics. Liberation-based politics are pursued by social groups that have found a voice in the late 60s and during the 70s and 80s. Some have antecedents and some have yet to shout out. Women, blacks, gays, people with disabilities, the young and old are among those who have been oppressed, discriminated against, and historically excluded from society at all levels. They have begun to find each other, sharing their common experiences and creating a different cultural life with different values from those of the dominant society. Some individuals within liberation-based political groups hold onto mainstream values and doubt the need to radically transform society. They want equality within the system, and so argue for social justice and equal opportunities. Nevertheless, they challenge the comfortable stereotyped attitudes traditionally held in 'Middle Britain' and are opening up the paths for further change, even without making fundamental change themselves. Others take a more radical stance and create the means to 'take control over their own lives' — control over their working situation, housing, culture, security etc.

The movement against nuclear power is an example of issue-based politics, which sometimes take in a single issue and sometimes a cluster. A nuclear power plant threatens the health of those immediately living round it: the security needed to police it infringes civil liberties; local ecological balance is disturbed; the society is committed to dependence on high-tech energy supply; and an older energy industry, coal, is placed in jeopardy. Here a coalition of groups with different interests could work together against the plant, each group with different areas of concern, often with conflicting views under the surface. However, working together can at least encourage understanding, if not agreement, on deeper questions. The peace movement has grown in response to the fear of nuclear weapons, but the people involved have broadened their activities and interests into other peace-related issues, including peace education, civil liberties, conversion of plant from military to civilian production, alternative defence, and creating friendship networks across inter-national borders. You need only look at the workshops at a peace movement conference to see the range.

People from liberation-based movements have become deeply involved in the issue-based peace movement, setting up their own organisations within the broader movement, getting their message across, providing distinct analyses of why we don't have a peaceful society and world. Most importantly, they have been challenging the way the peace movement reproduces within its own organisations and individuals, the very same characteristics of 'nuclear' society. Some have rejected these challenges, accusing the liberation groups of being divisive and even irrelevant to the 'central issue' of removing nuclear weapons. (For example, CND Cymru has had arguments about whether it should 'bother' to print a bi-lingual *Campaign Wales*.) Others have found the challenge difficult but personally stimulating, leading to a new awareness of aspects of their behaviour both inside and outside the peace movement.

All the new social movements have been consciously aware of the pitfalls of wishing to grow in numbers and influence, without developing a leadership out of touch with the grassroots, and of abandoning a practice where 'the personal is political'. Thus, they have attempted to evolve looser structures of organisation with a more equal relationship between constituent groups and individuals. Those schooled in centralised organisation would call it disorganisation. Small groups form a web-like network, with a criss-cross of relationships based on a specific action or project or area of interest. Sovereignty lies with the individual within the small group, based on the principle that 'those who do, decide'. The women's movement exemplifies this approach. There are no leaders and consequently no issues decided on by an elite group that will be the focus for the years' activity. There is no central fund or membership as such. Issues are taken up if there is genuine concern. Women decide what they want to work at and raise funds accordingly. The impact of the women's movement over a relatively short period of time has been tremendous, with repercussions in all areas of life, despite its apparent 'disorganisation'.

In some campaigns, decentralised and centralised organisational structures run side by side, sometimes they complement each other, at other times they are a source of conflict. For example, the animal liberation/rights movement has its older organisations such as the RSPCA and Animal Aid doing the parliamentary and welfare work and general education, while the Animal Liberation Front and Hunt Saboteurs Association, with a loose cellular structure, are more involved in direct action against animal abuse. The nuclear disarmament movement has CND, a large, visible and national organisation, producing publications and campaign materials for local groups, acting on campaigning priorities set by a huge annual delegate conference and a national executive committee. They also organise large demonstrations. Occasionally, the central organisation is out of step with the movement, sometimes having to be pushed along, and has borne criticism because of this. Local disarmament/peace groups, some of them in CND, have taken action on their own initiative, sometimes joining with other similarly minded groups and individuals. The countless actions at military bases, especially Greenham Common and Molesworth, the setting up of peace camps, the Stop the City action, Reclaim Chilwell, and Summit 8 have been organised largely outside CND.

Different movements have also co-operated on actions of mutual interest. The two mentioned above got together to hold a demonstration at Porton Down, where animals are abused in experiments to test military equipment.

A most important factor that binds the new social movements together (apart from such co-operative actions) is that there is an overlap of those involved in the various movements. People wear more than one hat, sometimes at the same time, sometimes trying one campaign after another. This proves to be an excellent means of direct communication, to complement the many publications, telephone trees, etc., that are spread across the movements.

The new social movements give less importance in their political analysis to control of the Nation State than the established Left and so their emphasis for action does not focus on the large and remote but concentrates on activities at a more local level and smaller scale. This has created the opportunity for experiments in new forms of living. Previously it was difficult to test socialism out to see if it worked simply because of the scale of the operation — it was all or nothing. Today there are hundreds of living experiments covering all aspects of a new society.

In the realm of work, co-operatives have re-emerged, with those involved directly responsible for whatever they produce or distribute. More communal forms of living are being tried in both urban and rural situations. Village-scale projects are in formation at Milton Keynes and Telford. Alternative Health Centres, providing a range of traditional and newer methods of health care, are springing up. There are small-scale educational projects for children concerned with the overall development of the child rather than moulding them to pass exams for a career.

Some people are educating their children at home. The alternative movement also provides many courses, usually at weekends, for adults.

Such projects are not simply experiments, and are not generally seen as such. They mainly express the desire of the participants to live a better life now, not wait until someone else does something on a grand scale. Here we have an alternative culture in the making, operating with different values from the dominant one.

The Role of Nonviolence

The undesirability of state power sidesteps the issue of whether social change will necessitate organised violence as an integral part of the strategy for change. Preparation for 'a crunch' involves creating sides, in which people are forced to make a choice, whether it is appropriate to their needs or not. Once the lines are drawn, it becomes much harder for individuals to find a way out of the situation and commitment becomes all or nothing. This sort of polarisation, which would still exist after state power had been seized, is a dreadful beginning for a peaceful, equitable, free and participatory society. The destruction leading up to the violent seizure of power would also serve as the *material* base for the creation of the new society.

Opening up possibilities for people to become involved in constructive projects largely outside the established framework of modern society undermines the role of violence, by providing an 'escape route' for those whose attitudes could harden into violent defence of the old order. In these times of transition into a 'post-industrial society', individuals are also in transition and become open to alternatives, especially when the future looks bleak.

These were some of the reasons the attention of radical pacifists in Britain during the early and mid 70s turned away from a pre-occupation with nonviolence as a technique for dealing with conflict towards nonviolent revolution, creating now the small beginnings of an alternative culture, a prerequisite for a peaceful society. They were also integrating the ideas of feminism and ecology into nonviolent revolution, just as anarchist and anti-imperialist ideas had been taken on board in earlier decades. They were still concerned about nonviolent action, but in Britain it wasn't until the controversy over nuclear power arrived, especially the proposed reactors at Torness, that

Opposition to nuclear power has grown. Here demonstrators nonviolently obstruct construction work at the site of Torness nuclear power station in 1980.

explicit nonviolent action, adopted by a movement, surfaced again outside of pacifist circles. (Ironically, an earlier generation of pacifists had argued in favour of 'Atoms for Peace' — the non-military application of nuclear technology. The double irony is that the purpose of the civil nuclear power programme was, in fact, to produce plutonium for the 'Atoms for War'.)

The Torness Alliance endorsed a tactical commitment to nonviolent action and used a small group approach to organisation, working alongside the more general Scottish Campaign to Resist the Atomic Menace. A major inspiration and influence on the anti-nuclear movement at this time had been the successful nonviolent libertarian occupation of a proposed nuclear power plant at Seabrook, in the US. The Seabrook action had been influenced by the campaign against the nuclear power plant at Wyhl in West Germany. The Torness Alliance didn't stop Torness being built, but it did draw people into contact with a radical community and its ideas. Other campaigns developed around different plants: at Windscale (now called Sellafield), the site of earlier protest, the opposition was revitalised; Safe Energy Groups sprung up in some cities and towns; campaigns to stop the dumping and transportation of nuclear waste developed; a proposed nuclear site at Luxulyan in Cornwall was dropped by the CEGB after a campaign of nonviolent action.

When NATO ministers decided, on December 12 1979, to deploy US cruise and Pershing missiles in Europe, thereby provoking a new peace movement, a radical constituency with a bent for nonviolent action was waiting in the wings. They came together with some of the nonviolent direct actionists of an earlier generation of anti-nuclear resistance. Nonviolent direct action has now become respectable within the peace movement, as people have seen and heard of the determination and spirit of the women of Greenham Common, peace campers at Moles-worth, the nuclear bunker success at Bridgend and the continuing struggle to halt the Carmarthen bunker, the war tax resisters and the 'Snowball' fence cutters. The peace movement is slowly developing from a movement of protest into a movement of resistance.

In all the new social movements, resistance and constructive projects combine to create a 'coin' with two sides — one side showing 'what we are against', the other side, 'what we are for'. Women resist male authority and violence in the family and create sisterhood in a women's collective household. Indian people resist the incursion of Western medicine into their community and create their own traditional practices. Black people find it impossible to get a loan from a white bank to set up a business, so they create a black-controlled bank. Young musicians resist the lure of the huge record companies and create their own record labels and distribution. And so on. A picture emerges of frustrated social groups evolving into social movements that are presenting a political and cultural challenge to dominant society.

A Green Umbrella

As an overall label that best represents a convergence in this melting pot of a new politics, I would hesitantly use the broad term 'green movement', to suggest that they all take their guiding principles from the narrower ecological movement. Many individuals in the new social movements would understandably reject this tag, precisely because it is associated with the ecological movement. However, the form of this political challenge displays some of the chief features of an ecological system. If you add together the principles of 'small is beautiful' and 'diversity is strength' and frame them into a holistic picture, you get something close to the new politics.

'Small is beautiful' is a reflection of the tendency towards small groups acting in predominantly local situations, with all individuals in the group equally responsible for its functioning. Diversity is evident, both in the range of groups *within* the movements and *between* the movements themselves. None is attempting to become *the* dominant movement. If one group or movement dwindles, then the whole is not seriously affected and there is room for others to join in without a power struggle. A holistic picture connects the movements and groups together, through the participation of an individual in a multitude of political activities with a broad awareness. The spiritual and holistic insight that 'we are all part of one another' is common to the movements and many individuals.

The Ecological Movement

The ecological movement proper has grown up in response to the industrial system, and how it deals with, or rather doesn't deal with, the twin problems of *depletion* and *pollution*. The

Organising in small groups is a more recent development in the peace movement. People who have just been deported from Denmark during the War Resisters' International Nonviolent March for Demilitarisation in 1985 greet each other.

problems are not new, nor peculiar to industrial civilisation — they even contributed to the Fall of the Roman Empire. But industrialisation, forged during the marriage between capitalism and the idea of scientific progress, has increased the magnitude of the problem tremendously. Critics of the industrial system are not new either — William Blake, William Cobbett and Robert Southey are early and vociferous British examples — nor is political activity against polluting industries. Concerns about health hazards to workers have been taken up by the trades union movement for many years, leading to the legislation of the Health and Safety Acts, ineffectual though these often are. The nuclear disarmament movement was deeply concerned in the mid 1950s about the effects of Strontium 90 (from atmospheric nuclear tests) in milk, and the effects of radiation on the survivors of Hiroshima.

In 1962, American biologist, Rachel Carson, wrote *Silent Spring*, drawing attention to the effects of pesticides on food and the local ecology. Round about the same time, the hippies in California, whose inhabitants consume more of the world's resources per capita than any other people, rejected the destructive, wasteful existence of their parents' generation and opted for a less materialistic and destructive lifestyle. During the 60s, their lifestyle found echoes throughout the Western world, as rich industrial societies (Britain was experiencing the 'white heat' of technology) were 'overdeveloped' in stark contrast to the 'underdeveloped' nations. By the end of the 60s, the cult had died down in Britain and the remaining hippies had lost their beads, but the issues still remained.

Experiments carried on, mainly in rural communes, to develop small-scale energy alternatives to the non-renewable fuels — coal, gas and oil. Wind, water, solar power and biogas fuelled the alternative technologies. Old tools were rediscovered and some improved. The 'alternativists' grew their own food without pesticides and chemical fertilisers, establishing a relationship with the land in contrast with commercial farming, which, since the Second World War, has become increasingly mechanised, using more energy to produce more food, but with more pollution and more depletion.

The alternativists were 'drop outs', usually university-educated, who, through choice, became marginal to dominant society. They proposed radical solutions to ecological problems from outside the system. At the heart of the system, the elite of global society, the industrialists, bureaucrats and their intellectuals also became conscious of the hazards to industrial growth. Their concern is genuine but, of course, they want to 'manage' the ecology in order to carry on business as usual. This top-down momentum of ecological awareness dates from 1970, when the Club of Rome, headed by an Italian industrialist and economist, published the influential if controversial *Limits To Growth*, concluding that the world could not support present rates of economic and population growth for the next two decades. The US report to Mr President, *Global 2000*, warned much the same in 1980. In 1972, the United Nations held an important Environment Conference in Stockholm that instituted the United Nations Environment Programme (NEP), addressing ecological problems at the global level. Following the quadrupling of the price of oil in 1973, Western governments were shocked into looking at alternative energy sources. The political and economic power of the OPEC cartel forced them to take more seriously the question 'What happens when the oil runs out?'

There have been a series of serious accidents that have also shocked — from oil slicks to radioactive leaks, from nuclear-test radiation to chemical plant disasters and liquified petroleum gas explosions. Flixborough, Aberfan, Seveso, Tory Canyon, Bhopal and now Chernobyl. Ecological problems are finally respectable. They are often worthy of serious study by governments and UN agencies, but only minimally acted upon.

Development and Ecology

One crucial question firmly on the agenda of global politics and asked by all nations is 'How do you develop with a minimum of pollution and depletion?' Western nations have partially solved this difficult problem by exporting it to the Third World. They have achieved this under the banner of 'development' by adding an ecological dimension to imperialism — eco-imperialism, if you like. Through their control of global production, Western industrialised nations are facilitating the shift of old industries (manufacturing, heavy industries, textiles, etc.) to the Newly Industrialised Countries, polluting urban areas in the Third World (crying out for a Dickens to come and make fiction of it). Multinational corporations are relocating the production lines for new industries to countries with sympathetic governments where land and labour come cheap, meanwhile retaining 'clean and white' research and development in the West.

Minerals and fuels in the Third World are not too carefully exploited, while in agriculture, Westerners import foods difficult to grow at home in December, and export Green Revolution-type programmes to compensate, making bigger farmers out of small ones, bigger profits selling seeds and fertilisers, and creating many unhappy people in the process. Similar processes operate in forestry and fisheries. The outcome of this is one of those stark facts — a third of the world's population consumes five-sixths of the Gross World Product.

Understandably, Third World peoples are sceptical of Western intellectuals' (radicals, liberals and conservatives) concern about global ecological problems. The message they receive is, 'Control your attempts to develop and for God's sake stop breeding so much, it only adds to the problem!' The Western model of development is responsible for this cruel mess. However, criticism is increasing within the Third World. Third World intellectuals have begun to link up with Western intellectual radicals through the agencies of the United Nations and organisations like the International Foundation for Development Alternatives, and are thus promoting participatory, self-reliant, appropriate and sustainable development projects all over the world.

In the West, the critique of development has also deepened. The twin problems of depletion and pollution inherent to industrialisation have become so serious that they have turned into an ecological critique of industrialisation, and the world-view that underpins it.

In Western philosophy, Arne Naess, a Norwegian philosopher drawing on Spinoza, Heidegger and others, has coined the term 'Deep Ecology' to signify a view of the world that says all living things, including humans, are contained in a total field, they are not separate from nature. This is distinct from 'Shallow Ecology' that deems humans superior and therefore set apart from the natural world. Practical application of these philosophical underpinnings would emphasise a co-operative partnership with other living things based on an equal relationship. Shallow ecologists would emphasise the sound management of nature with humans doing the managing in their position at the top of the 'natural' hierarchy.

The basis of scientific knowledge itself has been challenged by those in the leading science, physics, who reject the view of the material world as basically a mechanical system made up of building blocks. They argue that the sum of the blocks is greater than the parts, and that the parts aren't 'apart' but bound up in a totality. The evidence is from quantum theory and relativity theory. Fritjof Capra, in his book, *The Tao of Physics*, has equated this discovery with the mystical traditions of Eastern religions. Significantly, many young people who have turned away from materialistic values haven't turned to their own immediate tradition of Christianity or other Western religion, but have looked East or towards pre-Christian Western religions.

In economics, a small body of alternative economic thinking is grouped around The Other Economic Summit, a counter-institution to the Economic Summit of the leading industrial nations. The New Economics promotes: personal development and social justice; satisfaction of human needs; sustainable use of resources; and conservation of the environment. Alternative economic thinking is breaking out of the alternative movement, and although it is trying to diminish the importance of economic determinism and therefore the status of economists, it is being taken seriously by those not deterred by the political consequences of what has been called 'Buddhist economics'.

In production, there has been a slight trend away from the monopoly of mass-produced goods towards individually created goods of a higher quality and more durability. Although expensive, and therefore confined to those who can afford their product, the search for unique items has created a new community of craftworkers. The idea of Do-It-Yourself has also grown and isn't confined to the well-off — to some, it makes economic sense. You could dismiss this trend as a marketing trick, but it does indicate the desire for people to create their own homes. Some have even formed associations to co-operatively build their own houses, a once normal custom.

The idea of organic farming is more acceptable in the light of increasing public knowledge of the harmful effects of traces of pesticides in the food and water, and fertiliser run-off in the water. The Archers, that simple story of English country life on BBC radio, now has an organic farmer complicating the simple life.

Awareness of what we eat has become more important as a contributing factor to good health. Additives and pesticides are increasingly seen as dangerous to health, as are too much meat, sugar, salt, fats. The food industry is on the defensive and wholefoods and vegetarians are no longer confined to cranks and hippies. Wholefoods were even flavour of the month in gastronome circles, until nouvelle cuisine hit the scene.

In curative health, more people are turning away from Western medicine, usually in desperation, when their doctors and specialists cannot improve their condition. Acupuncture, homeopathy, reflexology, osteopathy, traditional herbal treatment, and a variety of alternative therapies are finding their way onto the high street, sometimes in alternative health centres.

Individually, these ideas and trends seem small beer (real ale?), seen together they carry an implicit, creeping critique of the value of life in a modern industrial nation.

The Acorns of Eco-Britain

In Britain today, the ecological movement has many facets. In the realm of parliamentary politics, the Green Party (ex Ecology Party) has found the justice rough without proportional representation. Nevertheless, it has become a national platform for putting forward radical proposals. The chief political criticism made about them has been the somewhat academic problem (as they have no MPs) of whether a party advocating decentralist anti-establishment policies should involve itself in a large-scale, establishment institution, i.e. Parliament.

The success of Die Grünen in West Germany has been achieved as far as I can tell, by 'walking on two legs' — the parliamentary leg complementing the extra-parliamentary leg of the social movements. The problems seem to have arisen later, when Left groups and others entered Die Grünen and democratically toned down their radical policies with more reformist proposals, tempted by a potential alliance with a larger party, the Social Democrats. The limitations of the parliamentary road to a 'green future' will become apparent, but to condemn such an attempt outright is meaningless. Such a road, in my view, has both strengths and weaknesses.

Meanwhile, in Britain, the major parties have become increasingly concerned with environmental issues and aware of the potential support of the environmental vote. The Conservatives have the Conservative Ecology Group, the Liberals, the Liberal Ecology Group, and the Labour Party, the Socialist

Environmental and Resource Association (SERA). SERA has worked within the trade union movement and influenced welcome changes in Labour Party and union policy. At the 1985 Labour Party Conference, following the adoption of an anti-nuclear energy policy by the Transport and General Workers' Union, the conference voted in favour of a resolution calling for a 'halt to the nuclear power programme and a phasing out of all existing plants'. SERA has been interested in the hybrid Ecosocialism, and has been instrumental in setting up a Red/Green dialogue, organising conferences with Green CND.

The more famous and general eco-organisations are Greenpeace and Friends of the Earth. Greenpeace is a transnational organisation largely involved in nonviolent action to highlight an issue and/or directly prevent such activities as Bomb tests and seal culling. Friends of the Earth acts as a pressure group, lobbying decision makers and educating the public, as well as implementing practical projects at the local level. Other initiatives include The Centre for Alternative Technology at Machynlleth and the Urban Centre for Alternative Technology in Bristol, which act as showpieces for the general public, largely for day visitors, demonstrating ecologically viable and practical alternatives. CAT also runs courses on alternative technologies and woodland management, organic gardening, and so on.

Groups such as Women for Life on Earth are bringing the ideas of women's liberation into the ecology movement and vice versa, while Green CND takes green ideas into the nuclear disarmament movement and vice-versa. The Henry Doubleday Research Association, Soil Association, and Permaculture Association are educating their members in less harmful ways of living, and are only some of the organisations working for a greener future. There are also the many, many people living ecologically more sensible lives, becoming less dependent on harmful technologies, trying to produce more of what they consume.

The ecological movement mustn't get trapped into solely forcing the polluters and depleters to manage their industries better. Its main focus, I hope, will be to work with the other social movements in organising more self-reliant, smaller scale communities, laying the basis for a more peaceful society.

Who Is Becoming Involved?

The overall impression of a highly complex network of small

groups (sometimes part of a larger organisation) is rather chaotic. It is very difficult to wind a way through the maze to pinpoint the state of this 'new society in the making'. Its weakness is its inability to be projected as a whole, and thus be offered to people as a simple alternative. However, as the problem isn't just a simple matter of registering a vote, but of encouraging people to become actively involved in stopping the torture of animals, confronting the verbal and physical violence dished out to blacks, women, gays, supporting boycotts, living more materially simple lives, transforming relationships and the rest, it can't come through the ballot box, only through personal contact and experience of new ways of behaving. This is often slower but more meaningful; the counting of heads is less important than the qualitative changes that people are making.

Those who have made radical changes in their lives, and some who haven't, must also remember that desirable changes cannot happen to others at the flick of a switch. Things take time, whether we like it or not. One real danger which I've come across several times is the difficulty of coping with 57 demands coming from an assortment of radicals *all at the same time*. It simply scares people and they retreat into their familiar experience. This wouldn't matter so much if the movements were solely concerned with creating a ghetto, but presumably we are trying to achieve broad societal change.

The appeal of alternative approaches, piecemeal at first, is to those who have time to include them in their consciousness. Those whose immediate issues of survival are obtaining food, housing, work, or whether they can safely walk the streets where they live have little choice. The 'choosers' are from the mildly disaffected middle layers of society. They can afford individual consumer choices, and may let nature provide a contrast to mechanical life in office and home by joining the National Trust to protect the countryside, or listening to and watching the wildlife programmes on TV and radio.

They may begin to realise a species of animal is being made extinct, so they send some money to Greenpeace and put a sticker on their car. Greenpeace have established some credibility with them as they have become 'counter-experts', suitable to make media comments. Such people were not initially fully convinced about Greenpeace's anti-nuclear stand, but they are impressed that Greenpeace *acts* from the highest principles, endangering their own lives in rescuing innocent seals, so there must be some validity to their objections. Then a nuclear accident happens in the Soviet Union and the wind blows radioactive clouds over Britain, where, as usual, it rains. Levels of radioactivity in the soil are higher than normal. The government says not to worry, it is not harmful, but advise farmers to halt the production of milk for a few days as the cows are eating mildly radioactive grass. Scientific idiots from the nuclear industry say it's something we've to learn to live with, there is no alternative to nuclear power, and besides their jobs are at stake. And so an environmentally concerned family is born.

They join Greenpeace or CND. They read *Greenpeace* or *Sanity* and find that there are horrendous things happening in the world, some of which they were previously aware of, but now see in a different light. The issues pile up and they may realise that their particular employment is tied up with this destructive culture. The main pillar of their survival, their relatively secure income, now comes under threat from their own crisis of conscience. They are ripe for the ecological movement, whether 'Deep' or 'Shallow'.

Those initial few from the bottom layers of society who become ecologically concerned will have a different conversion process, less intellectualised and more practical. They may, through lack of employment, join a radical building co-operative or join Women in Manual Trades or a similar group. Here they could become aware of small-scale brick production using rams, of plumbers taking an interest in solar heating and electricians in photo-voltaic cells. Or perhaps they are un-employed and wanting something useful to do, so they go round to the local Friends of the Earth/Green Centre and join in an insulation project.

Whatever their first contact, they will find it difficult to express in words what they think and feel, so will say very little. They won't understand the jokes, will experience being uninten-tionally ignored and made invisible, but won't quite know why. In their own social and family circles everyone is included, even strangers from another class. Hopefully they will meet with someone from a similar background to share experience and support each other. If not, they think of withdrawing. They will have less of a crisis of conscience, because they have less to lose, being lower down in the social structure. Their problem is whether they can survive in a semi-alien culture — a problem compounded by the lack of money.

This cultural clash has not really surfaced in the ecological movement yet, because the less privileged have not yet found each other, to then go on and challenge the more privileged. A non-Marxist class analysis needs to be integrated into the politics of ecology, and it is here that a Red/Green dialogue is important. The ecological movement has little direct experience of the problems of 'working class life'. The Left is at least familiar with some of the problems, even if it, too, is low on direct experience.

Many ecologists see the motive for an ecological commitment as primarily an *individual* revolt, not one of interests based around a certain class. This is perhaps due to the fact that the relationship between humans and their environment is the prime concern and there appears to be a greater likelihood of this relationship damaging everybody equally, at least, on the surface. The distinctions *between* human groups are easily lost when you think in terms of a species. Of course, class makes little difference to global ecological patterns in the chill of the nuclear winter or the heat of the greenhouse effect. However, if you can afford to move out of polluted cities, eat organic food, and have the best acupuncturist, some, as the saying goes, are more equal than others.

New Social Movements and the Left

In recent political history, the Left became the champion of the lower classes in their struggle for emancipation, and the workplace became the primary arena for class struggle. The new social movements have challenged these assumptions and, with varying degrees of sympathy, they have challenged the Left itself.

The political demands from the new social movements have influenced the Labour Party, particularly at the local party level, indeed some see them as the basis for revitalising the Labour Party and even Socialism. If the proponents of the 'new' socialism can break the hold of the social democrats within the Party, and win elections with a sufficient majority to carry out the sorts of policies and thinking we've seen in the recently abolished GLC and other metropolitan councils, this would undoubtedly be an important step in the short term. It could open up possibilities for the new social movements by providing resources and a platform and, most importantly, act as a line of defence to shield them from the pressure of the institutions of modern capitalist society.

The major problem is that one of these established institutions, the trades union movement, is right at the heart of the Labour Party, and historically gave rise to its existence, because the Liberal Party at the end of the 19th Century was unable to integrate the demands of workers and the trade union movement into its liberalism. I doubt whether the Labour Party could transform itself to such an extent that it would become a completely different party — no longer a *labour* party. The tension between the old and the new, which can also be creative, seems likely to run through the Labour Party for the foreseeable future.

In the longer term, the economic decline of Britain will force the political form of a national representative democracy into the shadows. Britain will exhibit the stark characteristics of many Third World countries — an elite tuned into the global economy, with a small sector of workers and security people servicing it, and the majority of people excluded, living a life of poverty and 'leisure'. There is one major difference however, and that is a large well-educated middle layer of society and an educated bottom layer. They are the products of industrial civilisation. They are going to have to organise and create a new existence in their communities or their lives will remain poor. Their 'poverty' will not be that of living materially simple, rich lives, but the alternative of destitution. The political domain will increasingly be at a more local level, where a more direct say in running the community is desirable and practical. This process will involve major social and political struggle, unevenly distributed and desperate for some. In short, a monied life will be exchanged for a more autonomous life, with survival being the motivating force for change. At best, the Labour Party could perform a useful transitional role.

The major difference between the new social movements and the labour and bourgeois challenges of past centuries is that they do not aim for control of national state power. The Labour Party (similar to other social democratic parties in Europe) have attempted to change capitalist Britain into a socialist system from within the established parliamentary institutions, which operate chiefly at the *national* level. They have succeeded in integrating the demands of labour into a 'social democracy' by reforming the capitalist system. (Some would say thus prolonging its life.)

Politics aimed at changes at the national level have also been the focus of the revolutionary Left. Their aim has been to force the contradiction between capital and labour into open widespread conflict, in the hope that the working class would win the day and instigate socialism, so that they could then dialectically dissolve into a classless society, communism.

The Communist Party, too, have felt the existence of the new social movements. There has been a serious split between those who favour a new communism, incorporating into Marxism the ideas of Eurocommunism and the new social movements, and the old guard, sticking to a pro-Soviet workerist Marxism. Those Left groups who haven't buried their heads in the sand have also been forced to examine their theoretical Marxism in the light of changed circumstances, and have added insights from ecological and feminist thought to their agendas.

Unlike the Marxist Left, and to a certain extent the Labour Party, the new social movements have not given supreme importance to the organisation of economic life as the determining factor for the rest of life. The elevation of economics to this pivotal position (capitalists do the same) is one of the problems of modern society. This is not to say that economic organisation is unimportant, indeed a major factor contributing to the current crisis in Western Civilisation is the state of the world economy. But remedies must put economic systems in the service of people, not the other way round. Many more systems of domination operate hand in hand with capitalism. Women have pointed to patriarchy, ecologists to industrialism, peaceniks to the war system, non-whites to white supremacy, mystics to unbridled materialism.

Together these critiques are influencing more and more people and are creeping deeper into the Western democracies, upsetting the 'natural' God-given authority of the white, middle-aged educated and rich male encased in his nuclear family, serving the nation state and its institutions. These sacred institutions are based on violence, both structural and direct. The new society attempts to create nonviolent structures, more equitable, self-reliant and smaller in scale, laying the basis for a less violent, more peaceful society.

* * *

Kenneth Boulding, a peace researcher, once remarked that the worst thing that could happen to peace is that it would become dull. In broadening its definitions of peace, *Peace News* through its history has helped create a *politics* of peace that has become more relevant. It has been able to support the new social movements as they have developed, finding common ground, and encouraging debate often at the risk of alienating the wider pacifist community. I, for one, think this alternative route has made peace far more interesting.

'Trafalgar Square was packed as tight as a bunny girl's bra . . .': Women's Issues in *Peace News*

by Lesley Mair

During the autumn of 1939, Mary Gamble encountered a lot of hostility to her idea that there could be a 'women's view' of the War, so much hostility, in fact, that she was prompted to write in *Peace News* on 12 January 1940 that '. . . I have come to suggest that the power lay in women's basic instinct for creation; but then I realized that that instinct is equally fundamental in man'. She then went on to say that the world was on a 'masculine rhythm and the feminine rhythm is stilled and submerged'. This was why she was troubled to see women in the uniforms of the armed forces. The piece ended with a quotation from Rainer Maria Rilke on the roles of the sexes. Mary Gamble's article was both prophetic and typical. It was typical of those entries which crop up occasionally, apparently without any context, say something fresh about women and nonviolence and then sink without trace only to find echoes many years or even decades later. Her notion of the 'masculine rhythm' does not resurface until the early 70s, the quotation from Rilke reappears again as a fitting conclusion to an article about sexual politics in 1973, and the whole question of women in the armed forces remains absent until it is briefly covered in 1978.

There is another feature about the coverage of 'women' in *Peace News* which distinguishes it from the other topics: the coverage alters dramatically under the impact of the women's liberation movement and the arrival of women in the collective. Although articles appearing after 1969/70 might deal with ideas first voiced by Mary Gamble, the basic understanding of women's place in the world was never to be the same again. Not that *Peace News* became a feminist paper. For a while in the early

70s the paper carried lots of reprints of articles on 'Women's Lib', but it was to be another five or six years before the implications of feminism for classic nonviolence really began to be talked about.

Together with the first pieces proposing that there could be such a thing as 'feminist nonviolence' came the first articles about an issue of central importance to both the nonviolent movement and the women's liberation movement. That issue was male violence.

Some pieces on Women's Aid in early 1974 had briefly touched on this subject when discussing the experience of some of the women in the refuges, who had been beaten up by husband or boyfriend. In May that year, six women closely connected with the paper had put together some pages on women's centres, women's papers and Women's Aid. (This was part of the paper's aim after the move to Nottingham to be a practical resource for those involved in local projects.) There followed reports in the following issues of events around Chiswick Women's Aid, one of the first, and the most widely publicised women's refuge at the time, run by Erin Pizzey. Perhaps because they could be regarded as factual reports about a self-help movement, these pieces seem to have caused few ripples. The main source of controversy was publication of an article by Penny Strange (19.7.74) called 'Do you think at your age it is right?' In it, she reflected on her mixed emotions at being touched up by an old man on a bus. She questioned why convention demands that 'old people' should not have any sexuality and why she felt repelled by it, yet at the same time she was angered by the presumption that there is nothing wrong in a man touching any woman's body. That controversy — provoking negative responses from many men, including several closely connected with the paper — soon merged into the general discussion about 'men against sexism' which was gathering pace at that time.

Apart from a spell in the late 70s, and three separate occasions in the 80s, male violence had not featured again in *Peace News*, a paper supposed to be concerned with all aspects of nonviolent revolution. Such discussion as there was in the 70s began on 22 April 1977, when *Peace News* ran an extract from *Against Rape: A Survival Manual for Women*, written in the USA by Andra Medea and Kathleen Thompson. (Susan Brownmiller's *Against Our Will* had already been published by Penguin, at a time when feminists had been making male violence one of their primary concerns for many months.) Shocked letters — are all men possibly seen as potential rapists? — followed along with letters from women wondering why men found it 'so hard to believe that women are sick and humiliated by approaches in the street'. The following May (1978) saw more feature articles on rape and the spread of rape crisis centres in many cities. The next significant article came on 3 October 1980, written by Jacky Brine and making a series of points, amongst them looking at police attitudes. This was at the time when the search was still on for the 'Yorkshire Ripper'. *Peace News* readers took this opportunity to 'think aloud' about rape in the columns of the paper and raised some interesting points about the rights of the accused, but judging from what was printed most focused mainly on just one issue raised in the article — women having to regard all men as potential rapists. Such was the volume of feeling on this issue that three women on the *Peace News* collective felt they had to publish their own rejoinder (12.12.80). *Peace News* covered the Women's Liberation Conference in Leeds on Sexual Violence (9.1.81) along with the establishment of Women Against Violence Against Women (WAVAW), and there the topic ended until an isolated article two years later, entitled 'Pornography — Violence Against Women' by Judy Greenway (22.1.82).

This piece was prompted by the discussion about pornography prompted by the publication at that time of books on the subject by two US feminists, Andrea Dworkin and Susan Griffin. It is a thoughtful and original article, but seems to have dropped like a stone. A short plea from Win Ashmore for men to stop moaning about feeling guilty and start organising themselves against violence against women has as yet not produced any visible reponse. That was in December 1983.

Another issue of crucial concern to both women's liberation and to pacifism is abortion. The editors of *Peace News* identified it more as a pacifist issue that concerned women than as a 'women's issue'. Needless to say, the subject was never discussed until 1967 at the time of the Abortion Act when letters appeared for and against abortion (from men and women). Some men defended abortion because they did not see more male contraception as a suitable solution. The moral dangers of The Pill were discussed. Two years later abortion surfaced again, this time in the 'John Ball' column. Normally this semi-editorial column, written on behalf of the paper by one member of the staff (after 1971) took a whimsical or satirical line. But sometimes it was perfectly straight. On this occasion it appears not to have been attempting satire, and took a strong anti-abortion line, arguing that the slogan 'A woman's right to choose' was no argument for abortion legislation because basically women were not capable of making such a choice. (Of course it was couched in less crude, more sociological terms, but that was the message.) Then in 1970 'John Ball' approached the subject from a different angle, comparing abortion and armed revolution, saying 'I have a similar though lesser sympathy for the person who sets up an abortion advisory service as I do for the guerrilla who shoots up a police barracks, which is to say a genuine sympathy, a degree of admiration and an essential rejection of the means being employed. A pacifist rejection' (7.8.70).

There was a two page editorial about abortion on 13 June 1975 opposing the White Bill then going through Parliament. It argued for a woman's right to choose and there were articles and correspondence on much the same ground in early 1980, when the Corrie Bill was similarly under debate. Once again there were men and women both for and against. August and September 1983 saw abortion spotlighted for a few weeks once more with the now familiar arguments rehearsed again: killing and control of sexuality, rights of the unborn, rights of women, freedom of choice, abortion as incompatible with nonviolence, the right of men to discuss the issue at all. By 1985 the debate had had to move forward to encompass in vitro fertilisation and experiments on the human embryo. A review by Penny Strange of the book *Test Tube Women* on 11 January 1985 provoked letters from readers with disabilities (or their mothers) questioning the use of abortion when genetic disabilities have been diagnosed before birth. Later in June that year two articles by Alison Davis and E. Treghenna shared the centre spread under the title 'Abortion and disability — whose oppression?' This looks like being, for the near future at least, the focus of the Great Abortion and Nonviolence Debate, and it is good that *Peace News* is at least reflecting some of the contemporary discussion about the control of the technology of reproduction, even if it is not breaking new ground.

If *Peace News* took (is taking?) a long time to make up its mind about abortion and is reluctant to tackle fundamentally the issue of male violence, this may be in large part because it has long had a very ambiguous position on the role of women. To illustrate: on 13 July 1962 the following went without comment: 'At the sports meeting of the Spadeadam rocket testing establishment at Brampton, Cumberland, the wife of one of the workers was elected "Miss Blue Streak".' If this 'spoke for itself' what did it say to the world which was to wait another eight years before feminists would disrupt the Miss World contest? *Peace News* time and again gave conflicting messages about women's role, on one hand describing and apparently approving of women's protest actions, whilst underneath, the basic assumptions about women's 'proper place' remained unchallenged. The following is a classic, and comes from a time when it is fair to say than *Peace News* should have known better. The front page, 1 October 1971, reported the demonstration by the Festival of Light (a right-wing backlash movement against the perceived dangers of the 'permissive society') and a counter-demonstration like this:

> Trafalgar Square was packed as tight as a bunny girl's bra with people who never appear for other demos about greater obscenities such as genocide in Biafra, Pakistan, S.E. Asia or unemployment and housing . . . Undoubtedly there was happiness for some of the participants, but this seems to have continued unabated while theatre groups from Gay Lib and Women's Lib were attacked by police and hustled off into paddy wagons . . .'

One month after the outbreak of the Second World War, a woman called Mary Taylor set off on a lone walk from Liverpool to London wearing a sandwich board with anti-war slogans. This inspired marches in London by women using the same slogans. Mary Taylor then called for mixed marches and more, new slogans. Something, it seems, was growing. However, John Barclay, then one of *Peace News*'s editors, oblivious to women's direct contribution, wrote on November 17 1939, 'I believe that the time is coming quite soon when every woman who has imagination and courage — and few are without either — will rise up and demand the immediate end to this most futile war. *It is all a question of a lead and that I propose to give.*' [Emphasis added.]

At this time the paper had no women editors, but could boast famous women contributors and (more often) reviewers — Vera Brittain, Ethel Mannin, Ruth Fry, Storm Jameson, Rose Macaulay and Kathleen Lonsdale, to name only the most well-

Liverpool Women's Peace March, February 1940.

known. Special mention must be made of Sybil Morrison, the most regular woman contributor who wrote for the paper from its earliest days until the early sixties (when it ceased to be the paper of the Peace Pledge Union). For almost two years in the early 40s she wrote a regular 'Women's Section' — a column mainly dealing with pacifist arguments based on women's role as mothers and citizens of the future, although it was her column (only) which gave what little coverage there was to the conscription of certain women for war work in factories and the armed forces in 1941. Despite this, when she was arrested and imprisoned in July 1940 for a speech made in Hyde Park, this was accorded a tiny paragraph on page 3.

An awareness that the dominant image of women in society prevailed to suit its needs seems to have been almost totally absent, though this awareness might have prompted *Peace News* to question, rather than slavishly reflect, the images of women desired by the status quo in the 50s and 60s. This period makes bleak reading for anyone looking for women *visible* as political activists rather than as mothers or potential mothers or girl friends carrying placards (supporting men imprisoned for refusing National Service) with the words 'I'm proud of my boyfriend in prison'. Of course, many strong women were playing an active role in their own right, organising and protesting, though not writing in or editing the paper. It remains as mothers, first and foremost, that women are seen and see themselves in these years.

Mary Gamble's reference to 'women's basic instinct for creation' finds echo upon echo in the 50s, 60s, and to an extent, in the early 80s. ('Creation' of course, referred to having children, rather than doing tapestry or inventing the transistor.) On 23 May 1947, the front page carried a plea from a German woman to all mothers to appeal with her for the release of prisoners of war still held, and the return of these soldiers to their mothers. By the early 50s this idea of universal mother-hood had evolved into mothers having a duty to save the world from the H-bomb and H-bomb tests, so that there would be a safe future for children. Allied to this was a recognition that men's age-long, self-proclaimed role as the 'protector' had come to an end. Civilians were now equally at risk of annihilation. (Vera Brittain first pointed out the erroneous nature of the myth of the 'protector' writing in *Peace News* a few days after the outbreak of the Second World War. The point was still being made in 1962, when Women's CND cited this fact as one of their reasons for founding their wing of CND.)

On 10 May 1957, the paper announced a forthcoming women's vigil and march at Westminster (calling for a halt to H-bomb tests) organised by the National Council for the Abolition of Nuclear Weapon Tests. Women were to be dressed in mourning. The report of this women's event the following week is telling: 'Mrs Collins reminded the audience that the marchers were ordinary women: housewives and mothers, not Communists or fellow-travellers, cranks or hysterical people.' This was not entirely true, as the audience included eminent scientists like Kathleen Lonsdale and other women with careers in their own right. The report continued,

> Loud and prolonged applause greeted Mrs Sheila Steele, whose husband had recently flown to India en route for the Pacific in a one-man [sic, although this is inaccurate] attempt to stop the British test. She told the crowd, 'We want a world where we can bring up our children safely and happily.'

As a woman, it seems, you could not possibly have political ideas as well. You were moved only by the argument that children needed to grow up safe and healthy and your only credentials were your husband's.

The idea that being a mother or potential mother precluded you from having any other analysis of war falls away during the 70s, only to re-emerge apparently unscathed, though not unchallenged, in the early 80s. Babies Against the Bomb came along almost exactly 20 years after Mothers Against War. But times *have* changed. *Peace News* readers would not now, I hope, allow to pass without indignant comment the only reference to a woman speaker at a rally being the fact that her husband had gone off on a 'one-man' (sic) attempt to stop the British test. Nowadays we do not all have to be mothers, and *Peace News* at least recognised that many women take political action on their own behalf, irrespective of whether or not they are, or intend to be, mothers. Meanwhile, the expectation remains entrenched in mainstream thought. If we are not going to *Peace News* on behalf of our children, we ought to be staying at home looking after them: the women who join peace marches or peace camps must by definition be bad mothers or worse — lesbian mothers!

The pages of *Peace News* have at times in the 80s been overflowing with coverage of women's peace actions at, around, or inspired by what began at Greenham Common in September

Chester Women for Peace on one of the Star Marches to Greenham Common, 1983.

Credit: John Harris

1981. Hardly a week has gone by for the last four years without some news or personal testimony by a woman of what it was like to blockade, to be arrested, to go to court, to live at a peace camp, and so on. In terms of sheer column inches, women's activities against Cruise and other nuclear weapons must be rivalling the coverage of conscription in the first few years of *Peace News*'s existence. The absolute hey-day for coverage of women's peace activities seemed to come in 1983, with a debate shortly after the preceding December's women-only 'Embrace the Base' action. The question everyone seemed to want to ask was 'Are women-only actions divisive and contrary to our understanding of nonviolent principles whereby no-one is ever excluded?' There are, of course, many other pertinent questions — such as whether women should fight the state's military power and aspirations, or whether we should put our strength into tackling our own oppression as we experience it directly.

Apart from some debate on the women-only issue in February 1983 and an analysis of the media coverage of the 'Embrace the Base' blockade, *Peace News* did not get to grips with most of the theoretical points raised by the sheer presence of large numbers of women abandoning the behaviour of decades and 'joining the peace movement'. For example, as 1983 wore on, and more women found themselves in prison, courtroom and prison experiences began to enter the paper. On 28 October, some analysis of the political and tactical aspects of going to prison were presented. Interestingly, this turned out to be a brief exposition of the theories about imprisonment put forward by two men, Gandhi and Martin Luther King. There followed some thoughts about 'why we fear prison and how to overcome these fears'. The piece ended, 'And so I do not think that those of us in a position to do so should feel that going to prison is a pointless activity, but rather be considering how to keep jobs and families together in spite of a few days inside.'

Feminists involved in nonviolent struggles have different analyses of what going to prison is all about, and an analysis of what made it so effective when MLK and Gandhi sought out suffering in this way. Traditional nonviolence holds that going to prison is a tactic for demonstrating the strength of feeling behind one's beliefs. The nonviolence involved in being incarcerated or beaten up for nonviolent action shows up the violence of the State in locking you up or beating you up. The more you are seen to suffer, the more the State should be shamed and its violence exposed. (For those whose nonviolence rests on religious belief the suffering is also redemptive because it is unearned.) The important thing is, of course, that the suffering and loss of liberty have been *sought*, and the point is entirely lost if the chosen suffering is not visible, not shocking, just part of mere existence. Thus many feminists argue that for women, physical and emotional suffering is rarely sought yet often found. Women's suffering carries less visibility and moral virtue. To seek imprisonment is a form of machismo, according to this analysis.

Feminists involved in nonviolence have been taking the opportunity to develop a feminist analysis of imprisonment as a nonviolent tactic. Feminist thinking on nonviolence in general has been published in *Peace News* too, as in 1978, when the paper reprinted several articles from *Shrew: Feminism and Nonviolence* (an issue of the now defunct feminist magazine, *Shrew*). The paper had actually printed its first feminist view of going to prison back in 1970 (3 July). As with much of the early writing on feminism and nonviolence, this came from the USA. Mary Moylan, the one woman among the Catonsville Nine,* wrote from underground in spring 1970:

> If I ever decided to go through Catonsville again, I would never act with men; it would be a women's action for me or I wouldn't act . . . I don't want to waste the sisters and brothers we have by marching them off to jail and having mystical experiences or whatever they're going to have . . . I think you have to be serious and realize you could end up in jail but I hope that people would not seek it as we did.

Although topics such as going to prison for nonviolent activism, women-only actions, abortion and male violence bring feminism and nonviolence into dialogue, they need not necessarily lead to a discussion of the nature of the connection between feminism and nonviolence. However, *Peace News* first speculated about this possible connection when it carried an exchange of correspondence (note: not articles) which ran for four issues, from 22

---

* The Catonsville Nine were a group of anti-Vietnam War demonstrators who destroyed draft files at a Selective Service office in a suburb of Baltimore on 17 May 1968. They went underground rather than be imprisoned when their appeals were rejected.

July to 26 August 1955. This looked at the application of 'pacifist principles' to 'women's struggles', and began with the question whether the suffragettes had used the wrong methods by espousing violence. Esme Wynne-Tyson argued that since 'emancipation' women had been degrading themselves by adopting men's unintelligent vices such as smoking, drinking, sexual promiscuity and 'going in for homicide' (she was referring to women in the Israeli Army) and that was all largely a result of having won the vote by the wrong means. Sybil Morrison, who had been active in the struggle for the vote herself, was quick to point out that the WSPU 'was not non-violent in the pacifist sense of the word, but it was an attempt at civil disobedience with a rigid regulation that no animal or human life should be endangered let alone attacked'. In reply, Françoise Delisle suggested that the vote had been ineffective perhaps because it was achieved 'in such objectionable ways'.

The next time feminism and nonviolence are so explicitly linked comes on 27 November 1970, when Betty Roszak reviewed Germaine Greer's *The Female Eunuch*. Roszak believed that Greer's book would anger 'those sisters of the orthodox Left' who would reject Greer's conclusions that the 'orthodox revolution with bombs and terrorism, their military discipline and hardness, hierarchies and regimentation are only more of the same bondage which women are struggling to free themselves from'. Roszak says that Greer's book naturally cannot give blueprints for this new kind of politics but does point a way to 'a revolution entirely new and different from all past revolutions'. Betty Roszak also took the opportunity of this review to dismiss, perhaps with hindsight too lightly, female freedom fighters. She admits that there are women who hold up a figure like Leila Khaled, a terrorist and guerrilla warrior, as a model, and who put posters on the wall of Israeli, Cuban and Vietnamese women carrying rifles. But these are only seen as 'proof that the masculine ideal of domination still holds these women in thrall'. Those of us who in the seventies considered ourselves nonviolent feminists found the 'thrall' had a great staying power, and that at that time the majority of the Women's Liberation Movement did not share our worries about the use of violent methods to achieve women's liberation. It is indeed a pity that in 1970 *Peace News* did not tackle in any depth the issues raised by those famous posters of the African woman with a baby on her back and a rifle in her arms.

An interesting look at the introduction of feminist awareness into a 'traditional' nonviolent struggle came on 5 April 1974, when *Peace News* published a two-page interview with Dolores Huerta of the United Farm Workers (extracted from *The Nation*, a US magazine). Huerta spoke of conflict she had had to deal with between her family (she had ten children and was divorced) and her commitment to the union's struggle: 'My biggest problem was not to feel guilty about it.' She described the early days when Cesar Chavez, keeping his machismo intact in those days, would make her, then his wife, come home and cook dinner. Women at this time were out on the picket line.

> The Teamsters attacked the line with 2×4 boards. I was in charge of the line. We made the men go back to the back and placed the women out in front. The Teamsters beat our arms but they couldn't provoke the riot they wanted and we didn't give in. The police stood there and watched us get beaten.

Interestingly there is no expression of surprise here that women being deliberately nonviolent got beaten, unlike the surprise at police violence felt by some at Greenham Common in the early days.

The following year, (21.11.75) *Peace News* published one of its many reprints from *WIN* magazine, 'Up From Under' by Andrea Dworkin, which addressed itself entirely to the connection between feminism and nonviolence:

> In my view, any male apostle of so-called nonviolence who is not committed body and soul to ending the violence against us is not trustworthy. He is not a comrade, not a brother, not a friend. He is someone to whom our lives are invisible. As women, nonviolence must begin for us in the refusal to be violated, in the refusal to be victimised. [I call on women to] establish values that originate in sisterhood. We must not accept even for a moment male notions of what nonviolence is.

Dworkin's article appeared at a time when sexism and feminism were, rightly or wrongly, presumed to be concepts understood by *Peace News* readers. For the preceding four or five years the paper had been giving coverage to the Women's Liberation Movement. After decades of covering the 'peace' movement in a narrower sense of the word, the pages of *Peace News* started in 1969/70 giving space to articles and reviews about feminism, yet Women's Liberation was presented as another form of liberation and almost in a vacuum, as far as *Peace News* coverage goes, as if it had no connection with the development of an analysis of nonviolence. In the early 70s, it must be said, *Peace News* was one of the few places such articles (and reprints) could find publication. The major women's liberation journal, *Spare Rib*, did not come along until 1972. By the mid-70s, the feminist press — magazines and newsletters — had got underway. One of the oldest of these was the magazine *Shrew*, put together by a different group of women round London and having a different theme each issue. The summer 1978 issue was on feminism and nonviolence and this edition was, in turn, the source of many reprints in *Peace News*.

The coverage of feminist nonviolence, like the coverage of many issues, has appeared in fits and starts. Looking back over 50 years of *Peace News* it is clear that one generation of editors and contributors has often been unaware of the earlier debate in the paper on the same issues. In this respect, the paper missed some good opportunities. For example, consideration of feminist thoughts on going to prison published in 1970 could have given a context to the reporting about imprisonment in the mid-80s. The paper was slow to learn from its own past coverage, even relatively recent past coverage. Such learning might have helped *Peace News* to make a new contribution, so that debates on male violence or abortion do not start afresh completely each time. *Peace News* also appears to have missed opportunities to comment on current events of particular relevance to the women and nonviolence question. There was no discussion, for example, of the implications of the establishment in 1938 of the Auxiliary Territorial Service (ATS, later Women's Royal Army Corps). Indeed, the only reference to the ATS was in 1948 when a conscientious objector called up to do National Service refused to put on uniform and was seen walking past an ATS barracks clad only in a towel! *Peace News* was similarly silent on the first ever issuing of guns to women in the armed forces in December 1980.

Despite omissions and fitful coverage, it is nonetheless possible to see some broad pattern emerging on the subject of women in *Peace News*. In the late 30s, women spoke as concerned citizens who, aware of having relatively recently obtained the vote, took very seriously their responsibility to contribute to national debate on international affairs. John Barclay's little faux pas reveals that this was not primarily the way men viewed them. In the early 40s, the 'concerned citizen' receded into the background and the paper's women contributors seem to have regarded their particular contribution to the pacifist struggle to be to try to mobilise ordinary women to make the war impossible by withdrawing support for husbands and sons at every level. They believed that in the mass of 'ordinary' women a strong anti-war instinct lay dormant and could be aroused by appeals to the womanly instincts. 'Their fundamental instinct for creation must rise in opposition to the destruction of life and everything that makes life worth living,' wrote Mary Gamble (5.5.39), just before the outbreak of war.

There is a marked dearth of contributions from women in the latter half of the 40s, as if nearly all energy was being poured into into relief work for children and refugees, although there is reference to a Women's Peace Campaign in 1949. Until this point, *Peace News* had never questioned the socially acceptable roles of women, and in the 50s it seems to have gone along wholeheartedly, if unconsciously, with the 'back to the home' ethos of the times. Housewives and mothers were to remain the stereotypes until the late sixties. The seventies saw enormous changes, not only in the pages of *Peace News* and in the addition of women to the editorial side of the paper, but in society as a whole. Whole new areas were opened up for discussion. Towards the end of the decade, *Peace News* had begun to move from regarding women's liberation as another 'right-on' cause, to some initial reflections on the implications of feminism for nonviolence as a whole.

And the 80s? A trend seems to be emerging in the *Peace News* of the mid-80s of making explicit links between previously distinct topics — women *and* nuclear disarmament *and* world poverty and development *and* miners wives (following the strike of 1984/5). The future is open — hopefully there will still be room for these prophetic voices.

Liberation and Development: Gandhian and Pacifist Perspectives

Geoffrey Ostergaard

'Liberation' and 'development' denote two major themes in the politics of the post-war world. But are they matters which concern pacifists qua pacifists? Perhaps not, according to the common perception of pacifism. Except, of course, when liberation movements take to armed struggle and 'internal wars' result. Then pacifists should be concerned, since for them all war is 'murder done to the sound of trumpets'. But not all liberation movements involve war, and no such consideration attaches to issues of 'development'.

I wish to suggest, however, that the two are of integral concern to pacifists, at least to those whose pacifism is of the kind expressed in *Peace News*. And they have become so over the last fifty years largely, though not wholly, through the influence of one person — M K Gandhi. Gandhi's philosophy of nonviolence has helped to transform pacifism so as to render old-fashioned and inadequate the common perception. From being a specific doctrine about war (or, more accurately, being perceived as such), pacifism has changed and is on the way to becoming a comprehensive ideology with a worldview. In the process, pacifists have developed perspectives on liberation, development, and a variety of apparently non-pacifist matters, as other chapters in this book also illustrate.

Gandhian perspectives on liberation and development

The popular perception of Gandhi as 'the Father of the Nation' who won independence for India by using the technique of nonviolent resistance which he called 'satyagraha' is not incorrect, but it is seriously deficient. Gandhi certainly did a great deal to foster the concept of India as a nation, by mobilising the masses and involving them in politics — politics of a special kind centred on nonviolent action. Gandhi, of course, was not the first to use this mode of action, even in India. But he broadened and refined the technique, demonstrated how various were its methods, and persuaded the Congress to adopt it as the main element in its strategy for national liberation. In the course of a series of nationwide campaigns — the Rowlatt Satyagraha, 1919, the Non-Co-operation Movement, 1920–22, the Salt Satyagraha, 1930–31, and the 'Quit India' Movement, 1942–44 — millions of Indians protested against alien rule and refused in various ways to continue co-operating with it; and many thousands went further, committed acts of civil disobedience, and filled the jails. As a result, the national political community was vastly extended and strengthened.

But Gandhi's nationalism was of a benign kind, fully compatible with his universalistic belief that all human beings are primarily members of a single family — the human race. No particular section of this family could be free while subject to the rule of other sections. The national liberation of all subject peoples was, therefore, necessary, but only as a step towards the larger goal of the liberation of humanity.

The term Gandhi himself used for 'liberation' was *swaraj*, connoting freedom, autonomy, self-determination and self-government, but not just in a political sense. The liberation he sought was total and expressive of an integral philosophy of life. This philosophy was grounded in the Indian tradition of thought, a central belief of which is that a principle of unity underlies the cosmos, linking humans, animals and the natural world in a single whole that is fundamentally spiritual. Liberation, therefore, had other dimensions besides the political: spiritual, ethical, economic, social and cultural. As a devout, if unorthodox Hindu, Gandhi gave primacy to the spiritual. The liberation he sought was in the first place his own: release of his particular self through its identification with the universal spirit — the process of self-realisation, which he equated with God-realisation. But, unlike the typical Indian fakir, Gandhi did not pursue it as a solitary quest. He believed that his own spiritual liberation could not be achieved apart from the liberation of all other human beings, and that the way to pursue it was through service to others, especially the oppressed.

Liberation in all its aspects tied in with 'development',

construed not in its current narrow sense but as 'human growth'. And the two proceeded together. As individual human beings, in the company of others, pursued liberation, their natures, part animal but also part divine, would be transformed by their increasing insight into reality — what Gandhi called Truth, the obverse of which is Nonviolence, or Love. The values they lived by would change; the new values would be expressed in institutional forms; and they would proceed to revolutionise totally, but nonviolently, the arrangements of their communities. Gandhi's concept of Satyagraha — meaning literally 'the firm grasping of Truth' and not, as commonly translated, 'nonviolent resistance', — encapsulates his philosophy of action; and his concept of Sarvodaya — 'the raising up and the welfare of all' — encapsulates the goal.

That this was Gandhi's 'mission', and what accepting his 'message' implied for human society, is suggested by a reading of *Hind Swaraj*, the booklet he wrote in 1909 while serving his 'apprenticeship' in South Africa. In it, he took issue with India's violent revolutionary nationalists. They mistakenly assumed that India had lost her freedom because she had been violently conquered by the British, who must, therefore, be driven out by violent means. He argued:

> The English have not taken India; we have given it to them . . ..
> Some Englishmen state that they took and hold India by the sword. Both these statements are wrong. The sword is entirely useless for holding India. We alone keep them . . ..

In these words, Gandhi expressed his belief in the theory of 'voluntary servitude' which he had learned from Tolstoy. The theory, which constitutes the intellectual foundation of nonviolent action, maintains that, despite appearances to the contrary, structures of power which divide humans into rulers and the ruled, exploiters and the exploited, do not in the last analysis depend on physical force exercised by the dominants. They depend, rather, on the co-operation, freely or reluctantly given, of the people who are dominated. If that co-operation is withdrawn, structures of power must inevitably crumble. Real power always resides in the people. The problem, of course, is that this power is usually latent. To be effective, it has to be organised and manifested in action.

The bulk of *Hind Swaraj*, however, is devoted not to expounding his concept of satyagraha but to a critique of modern, that is, Western civilisation. In a judgement that clearly reflected the influence of John Ruskin's *Unto This Last* and Edward Carpenter's *Civilization: its Cause and Cure*, Gandhi severely condemned Western civilisation which he likened to 'a deadly upas tree'. Fundamentally, it was godless and immoral, indeed, 'Satanic'. Its dynamic principle was a materialism which encouraged the quest for physical comforts but not the satisfaction of real human needs, and certainly not spiritual and moral growth. At its centre was industrialism. Industrialism had led inevitably to the concentration of power in the hands of the few, while the bulk of the people had been herded into cities where they were employed in factories and reduced to being little more than slaves to machines. Industrial civilisation was inherently exploitative and enslaving. It had enslaved the British themselves and it was the root cause of the enslavement of India, where the educated elite had been corrupted by its false values.

Part of Gandhi's object in writing *Hind Swaraj* was to remind his own people of the strengths and virtues of traditional Indian civilisation, but there is no doubt that he was deeply convinced of the treacherously deceptive and self-destructive tendencies of Western industrial civilisation. Striking an ominous note, he observed: 'This civilisation is such that one has only to be patient and it will be self-destroyed.'

In Gandhi's view, the colonial policies of Western states were a product of their industrialism. Political domination of the colonised countries facilitated their economic exploitation. The colonies were treated as the source of raw materials for factories in the imperial countries where they were made into finished goods mainly for sale in colonial markets. In the process, the traditional local, largely self-sufficient economies of colonised countries were either destroyed or seriously disrupted. India provided a glaring example. Its once-flourishing cottage industry of hand-made textiles, second in importance only to agriculture, had been virtually destroyed. As a consequence, unemployment and poverty had increased, village economies had been thrown off balance, and the communities based on them undermined. The solution to the problems could not, however, be found by India becoming an industrial state on the Western model. That would still leave the villages — 'the real India' — exploited by the cities, even if Indian rather than British ones. And it would mean India itself joining the ranks of the exploiting nations. The solution was to be found, not in mass production, located in cities, with dehumanised workers using machines owned by others, but in production by the masses, in the villages, with people using tools they themselves owned and controlled. In short, the solution was to be found in the spinning wheel, the *charkha*. Not, of course, in the instrument itself, but in all that it symbolised for Gandhi.

For him, it symbolised many things. Village industries and crafts that could provide work for unemployed villagers, making unnecessary their migration to the cities. Simplicity in living. This was not to be identified with poverty, which was a great scourge that had to be, and could be, eliminated. For, as Gandhi put it, 'There is enough in the world for man's need, but not for his greed.' The *charkha* also symbolised the importance of 'bread labour' — the idea that everybody, in earning their daily sustenance, should work at least part of the time with their hands, thus overcoming the age-old division between mental and manual labour. Further, it symbolised an economy based on the principle of *swadeshi*. Originally this meant the boycott of foreign-made goods; but Gandhi extended its meaning to embrace self-reliance and self-sufficiency. Self-sufficiency did not imply complete economic independence. Interdependence was an inescapable and also welcome act of life. But it did imply that each local, as well as national, community should be capable of meeting its basic material needs. Beyond the economic, *swadeshi* implied a way of serving the world through serving one's local community: 'It is the spirit in us which restricts us to the use and service of our immediate surroundings to the exclusion of the more remote.' Again, the *charkha* symbolised the need for creative self-expression, and the satisfaction that comes from making objects of real use to people. And, not least of all, the *charkha* symbolised a non-exploitative technology.

Gandhi's condemnation of the machine — his term for technology — was open to misinterpretation. Without retracting the main thrust of *Hind Swaraj*, he later made his position clearer: 'There should be no place for machines that concentrate power in a few hands and turn the masses into mere machine-minders, if indeed they do not make them unemployed . . . there would be no objection to villagers using even the most modern machines and tools they can make and afford to use.'[1] It was not technology as such that Gandhi objected to, but industrialism. Industrialism had been the product of capitalism, but, again, capitalism as such was not the root of the problem. Hence, simply replacing capitalism with socialism would not solve it. Perceptively, he observed, 'Pandit Nehru wants industrialisation because he thinks that if it is socialised, it would be free from the evils of capitalism. My view is that the evils are inherent in industrialism and no amount of socialism can eradicate them.'[2]

The promotion of *khadi* (handspun, handwoven cloth) became the best known item in Gandhi's Constructive Programme. It comprised eighteen items but the list was open-ended, and one item, economic equality, was described as 'the master key to nonviolent independence'.[3] The underlying purpose of the Programme was the rehabilitation of Indian society, without which, in Gandhi's view, *swaraj* could not be attained or have real meaning. In present parlance, it was his practical programme for development.

It reflected also the positive face of nonviolence. Nonviolent resistance to the British, though necessary, reflected the negative face. He believed indeed, that if workers made a success of the Programme, independence could be achieved without civil disobedience. However, towards the end of his life, Gandhi confessed that he had got his priorities wrong: fearing to estrange co-workers, he had placed civil disobedience before constructive work. The nonviolence displayed in the independence struggle, he concluded, had been largely that of the weak, not the strong. 'Nonviolence of the weak' was Gandhi's phrase for 'pragmatic', as distinct from 'principled', nonviolence — adopted because violent weapons are not available or because their use, in a particular struggle, is judged inexpedient. Although his own nonviolence was 'principled', he had promoted nonviolent action as a 'policy', rather than as a 'creed', in the belief that it would be effective as a policy, but also in the hope that its adoption as a policy would lead to its acceptance as a creed. In the event, his hopes were largely dashed, and at his death he left unresolved the vexing issue of the relationship between pragmatic and principled nonviolence.

It is clear, however, that Gandhi did not regard nonviolent action merely as a political technique. 'Technique' suggests a framework of thought in which means are separable from ends. This framework has become dominant in the West in modern times but it is not Gandhi's framework. He saw human action as a continuous process in which ends and means are distinguishable temporally but not morally. This implies that means are never merely instrumental; they are also always expressive of

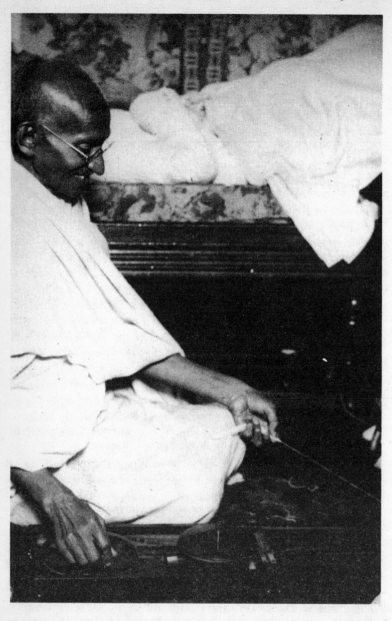

Gandhi spinning on board the cross channel steamer as he travelled to the round table conference in London in 1931.

Credit: Associated Press

values: ends-in-the-making. The relationship between the two is not technical but, like seed and tree, organic. And, since one can never be sure of attaining one's ends, one should concentrate on means, which are within one's control. Then, if the means are pure, the end-result will coincide with the end-goal.

Because the Constructive Programme represented Gandhi's positive means, it pre-figured his end-goal: the Sarvodaya society. Since the state is 'violence in a concentrated and organised form',[4] Sarvodaya is a stateless society in which all political and legal authority have been abrogated, relations between people being governed only by moral authority. Structurally, it is 'a great society of small communities', each autonomous and self-governing but linked with others in a non-hierarchical network — part of an 'oceanic circle', to use Gandhi's more vivid image. Internally, each community is a participatory democracy, taking decisions by consensus, so that individual and collective self-government coincide. Each community is self-sufficient in meeting its basic needs for food, clothing and shelter. Agriculture is the main occupation, but there are various other small-scale industries, organised co-operatively and using a technology that serves human needs. Any large-scale industry that may be necessary is organised on a federal basis. Private property in the capitalist sense and public property in the state socialist sense do not exist. Instead, the principle of trusteeship prevails: all property, however 'owned', including the natural talents of individuals, is held on trust for the service of all. Economic equality, interpreted to mean distribution according to needs, is the rule, and the society is classless. But equality is combined with respect for freedom of the individual — the person at the centre of the 'oceanic circle'.

The Sarvodaya society is, of course, an ideal society and, like all ideals, it may never be fully realised. But it indicates the direction in which, so Gandhians believe, Indian society and, eventually, societies throughout the world, should move. The Sarvodaya society, it should be noted, resembles that visualised by libertarian socialists, such as the Owenite co-operators, the Russian populists, and Kropotkinian anarchist-communists. It is located squarely in the tradition of 'village communism' which contrasts sharply with Bolshevik Communism. 'Communism which is imposed on people', wrote Gandhi, 'would be repugnant to India. I believe in nonviolent Communism . . .. If

Communism comes without any violence, it would be most welcome.'[5]

'Without any violence' implied, in Gandhi's view, that development should proceed from below and not be directed from above by the state. Hence, on the eve of his assassination, 30 January 1948, he proposed that the Congress, having attained political independence, should disband as a political party and become a constructive work organisation with the task of achieving 'real swaraj' for India's villages. The proposal was rejected and, instead, the Congress, with Nehru waving the banner of democratic state socialism, sought to develop India as a modern, industrialised nation-state. It was left to a few thousand constructive workers, led by Vinoba Bhave and Jayaprakash Narayan, to pursue Gandhi's strategy. This they did through campaigns for Bhoodan (landgifts) and, later, Gramdan (voluntary villagisation of land), the emphasis, until 1974, being heavily on constructive, rather than resistive, nonviolence. As a result of the campaigns, in the course of which they elaborated Gandhi's concept of nonviolent revolution, half a million landless labourers were given land and a few thousand Gramdan villages have begun to develop in the Gandhian way. But the overall impact on the wider society has been limited and, today, Gandhi's vision of an India of village republics remains largely a dream.[6]

Meanwhile, in the Eighties, India has emerged as the tenth largest industrial state in the world, although three-quarters of its 700 million people still live in villages, with agriculture as their main occupation. With occasional genuflections to 'the Father of the Nation', India adopted 'the conventional development strategy'[7] followed in most Third World countries. Between them, the 'advanced' countries of the capitalist West and the socialist East have provided the model. The accent has been on economic development and 'modernising' the economy. It has involved building up large-scale heavy industries that are bureaucratically controlled, inefficient, and capital-intensive. When capital is scarce and labour abundant, this makes little economic and no human sense. At the outset, Nehru declared that large-scale industry would be developed in tandem with agriculture and village industries. But the actual allocation of development resources to the rural sector in the period 1951–66 never exceeded fifteen per cent; and, in those years, although agriculture contributed half the national income, it obtained only one per cent of the foreign aid to India. Subsequently, after famine in Bihar, more resources were allocated to the rural sector and, in recent years, India has become self-sufficient in foodgrains. But the thrust of development in the rural sector, most noticeable in areas of the so-called Green Revolution, has been towards turning agriculture into a modern, mechanised and capitalist industry, its production geared to supplying food to the cities on terms that favour consumers rather than producers. Despite the Government's land reforms, the class of landless labourers, which the Sarvodaya movement had sought to abolish through Bhoodan and Gramdan, remains, constituting one-third of the rural workforce.

The cities, swollen in size by mass migration from the countryside, have become increasingly unmanageable. The poor live in festering slums and shanty-towns, in conditions contrasting sharply with those in middle class suburbs. In India, as in other Third World countries, development has led to the emergence of a 'dual economy'. Islands of 'modern economy' exist in an increasingly turbulent sea of 'traditional economy'. The idea behind the 'conventional development strategy' was that new wealth would be generated which would then 'trickle down' to the poor, raising their living standards and stimulating further change. But little has trickled down. As measured by per capita Gross National Product, the key index of the strategy, living standards have improved since independence. But, in broad terms, what has happened is that the rich have become richer and the poor have remained poor or, in some cases, become even poorer. According to the Government's own criterion, at least one-third of India's citizens exist below the poverty line.

The failure of the Government's strategy to improve the lives of the masses was one factor — along with difficulties in implementing Gramdan and Indira Gandhi's dictatorial tendencies — which led the Sarvodaya movement in 1974 to change course radically. Its activists joined Jayaprakash Narayan in promoting a 'people's movement' which engaged in mass nonviolent resistance of the kind used against the British Raj. The confrontation provoked Mrs Gandhi into imposing a repressive state of emergency on the country from 1975–77, which ended with the electoral defeat of the Congress by the

Janata (People's) Party. The Janata Government pledged itself to promote 'Gandhian socialism' but, faction-ridden, it fell apart before significant steps were taken to apply its 'alternative development strategy', which involved giving priority to agriculture and small-scale industries. After Mrs Gandhi's return to office in 1980, there was a return to the previous strategy. Under Rajiv Gandhi, rural development is receiving more attention than before but, as his speech on the 38th anniversary of independence indicated,[8] he believes that science and technology provide the key to India's future. His rider that the technology would be 'indigenous and suited to the country' may be taken as the polite bow most Indian politicians make to the ideas of his namesake, M K Gandhi.

Pacifist perspectives on liberation and development

In turning to pacifist perspectives, as reflected in *Peace News* over the past fifty years, it is necessary to relate them to three phases in the development of pacifism. The phases are not sharply separable but each is characterised by a *predominant* orientation. In the first phase, 1936–51, the orientation is on pacifism and peace-making as commonly understood, with liberation and development scarcely figuring as pacifist issues. In the second phase, covering roughly the next fifteen years, the orientation is on nonviolent action as a technique that can be used not only in the cause of war resistance, but also in struggles for liberation. In the third and continuing phase, nonviolent revolution becomes the predominant orientation. (The orientation of the third phase is reflected in the journal's subtitle, 'For Nonviolent Revolution', which was adopted in 1971, although the orientation is clearly discernible from the mid-Sixties.)[9]

In the first phase, attention is focused on what are usually regarded as the distinctive issues of both pacifism and pacificism. The latter term connotes the broad movement that seeks the abolition of war and the creation or maintenance of peace through disarmament, the use of arbitration and conciliation, and the strengthening of international law and organisations. Pacifism has the narrower connotation implying, in addition, personal non-participation in war, as exemplified in conscientious objection to military service and the PPU pledge. The underlying assumptions of both are that war is the supreme evil and that it can be eliminated by states adopting new norms to regulate their behaviour towards each other, pacifists adding that individuals must also adopt new norms and refuse to take part in organised killing.

From the Gandhian perspective, a pertinent critique of this orientation was made by Bharatan Kumarappa in 1949:[10]

> The underlying motive of pacifism is negative, viz. the avoidance of war. As against this, Gandhiji's conception is fundamentally positive. His nonviolence is not a weapon to be used merely to prevent war. It is, on the contrary, to enter into the very fibre of one's being and revolutionise all sides of one's life — individual, domestic, social, political and economic . . . While pacifism hopes to get rid of war, Gandhiji goes much deeper . . . . (His) cure is . . . very radical . . . . It demands nothing less than rooting out violence from oneself and one's environment . . . . It involves much self-restraint and renunciation, while the whole tendency under modern industrial civilisation is towards self-indulgence and the multiplication of wants. Western pacifists wish, as a rule, to maintain their standard of living and are not prepared to lower it in any way. All they seek is some way of doing away with war, without changing in the slightest their mode of life.

Kumarappa's criticisms were not wholly justified. Dick Sheppard, founder of the PPU, had pointed out that pacifism was 'something more positive than a renunciation of war', the elimination of which was 'but one step in the construction of a wiser, saner and more humane social order.'[11] Other leading British pacifists had made the same point, even more strongly.[12] And Bart de Ligt, the Dutch anarchist, anti-militarist, and critic of 'bourgeois pacifism', had outlined a strategy for nonviolent revolution to rid the world of capitalism and imperialism — the root causes of war.[13] Kumarappa's criticisms, therefore, may be taken to apply more to pacificists than to pacifists. But in a period when socialist pacifism was on the defensive within the Labour Movement, and the PPU was organising on the basis of its pledge, even pacifists did not succeed in projecting clearly to the public the idea that abolition of war was integrally linked with fundamental social changes.

The situation began to change when 'nonviolent action' became the predominant orientation. Signs of this began in the preceding phase as pacifists, some of whom had earlier looked askance at Gandhi's methods, came to see their relevance. In 1935 Richard Gregg published *The Power of Nonviolence* which expounded Gandhi's technique. The book persuaded many pacifists that pacifism could provide an alternative to war and that it possessed what Huxley described as 'a technique of conflict — a way of fighting without violence', and one that is 'unquestionably effective'.[14] For a few years prior to the Second World War, 'Greggism' was a lively current of *thought* in PPU groups. But nonviolent action remained at that level and it was not until after the war that a new generation of pacifists took it further. In 1952 they organised 'Operation Gandhi', the first nonviolent demonstrations against nuclear weapons in Britain. Five years later they formed the Direct Action Committee Against Nuclear War, which helped to spark off the Campaign for Nuclear Disarmament, and which later merged with the Committee of 100. In this way, radical pacifists, using the technique of nonviolent action, broke out of their 'ghetto'. They found themselves addressing larger audiences; they exchanged ideas with other radicals; they joined with them in confronting the state; and radical pacifism became a significant tendency in the emerging New Left.

In essence, what pacifists did in this period, as far as Gandhi is concerned, was to abstract from his work a technique, largely ignoring as irrelevant his metaphysical, moral, political, social and economic ideas. The general attitude was summed up by the anarchist, Nicolas Walter, in *Nonviolent Resistance*, 1963:

> Gandhi linked many things to satyagraha which aren't essential to it. His religious ideas (non-possession, non-acquisition, chastity, fasting, vegetarianism, teetotalism) and his economic ideas (self-sufficiency, 'bread labour', and agrarianism) don't necessarily have anything to do with post-Gandhian nonviolence.

Pacifists were more aware than Walter of the importance Gandhi had attached to constructive work, but even they tended to see it as an adjunct to nonviolent resistance, overlooking that his Constructive Programme was the positive expression of nonviolence and carried intimations of the Sarvodaya society.

It is rather ironic that pacifists in the West discovered the importance of Gandhi's technique at a time when the Sarvodaya movement in India, under Vinoba's guidance, was emphasising constructive nonviolence and downgrading 'negative' satyagraha. Through *Peace News*, pacifists were kept informed of the progress of the Bhoodan-Gramdan campaigns, but with few exceptions, such as Wilfred Wellock, they did not see the Sarvodaya movement as pursuing a strategy which had implications for other developing societies and also their own. On the whole, they were less captivated by Gandhi's 'spiritual heir', Vinoba, than by his 'political heir', Nehru, with his programme of modernisation and his efforts to build a bloc of 'neutralist' states.

However, pacifists did see that nonviolent action had wide implications. British pacifists employed it first in a recognisably pacifist cause, even if some pacifists were unhappy about the emphasis on nuclear, rather than total, disarmament. But the technique, like its military counterpart, was deemed to have universal applicability, at least potentially. It could be used to right any wrong, combat all oppression. In the USA at this time, the Civil Rights Movement, led by Martin Luther King, was using it effectively in the struggle of the Blacks. Gandhi, of course, had used it to gain India's independence; and, since the liberation of other colonial peoples was now high on the agenda, it was to this issue that pacifists gave increasing attention. In doing so, they were giving fresh impetus to the anti-imperialist tradition of the No More War Movement, an organisation of socialist pacifists which had merged with the PPU in 1937 and one of whose members, Fenner Brockway, now a pacif*ic*ist rather than a pacifist, had founded the Movement for Colonial Freedom. But they were also encouraged by the fact that several prominent African nationalist leaders, among them Nkrumah, Kaunda, Nyerere and Luthuli, regarded the struggle led by Gandhi in India as the exemplary model.[15] In the Gold Coast in 1949, Nkrumah launched a campaign of 'positive action' which he later described as employing 'the weapons of legitimate political action... and, as a last resort, ... strikes, boycotts and non-co-operation based on the principles of absolute nonviolence, as used by Gandhi in India.'[16] The campaign helped to hasten the granting of independence in 1957 to Ghana — the first new African state. Nonviolent action also played a role in the struggles in Nyasaland (Malawi) and Northern Rhodesia (Zambia) but not in Kenya, where the obduracy of the white settlers provoked the violent Mau Mau uprising. British pacifists added their weight to campaigns in this country to press the Government to speed up the granting of independence, and *Peace News*, under Hugh Brock's editorship, devoted considerable space to African affairs and carried a regular column written by Fenner Brockway.

But they also did more. Some felt it incumbent on pacifists to intervene directly in the struggles in order to demonstrate solidarity with colonial peoples and to provide training in the technique of nonviolent action. This they did through the World Peace Brigade (WPB), set up in 1962 by War Resisters' International, whose British, American and Indian sections provided the main support.[17] The ambition of the new organisation was 'to bring the liberating and transforming power of nonviolence to bear more effectively in our world'. Its first major project, conducted under the auspices of an alliance of African parties, was to take part in a march from Tanganyika into Northern Rhodesia, in support of a general strike that Kaunda threatened to call. In the event, the march was called off when Kaunda decided to participate in elections and pursue the path of negotiations that led finally, in 1964, to Zambian independence. The WPB sponsored two other projects before it quietly expired: *Everyman III*, a boat which sailed from London to Leningrad in September 1962, to protest against Russian nuclear tests, and the Delhi-Peking Friendship March, organised after the Sino-Indian border war of 1962, but abandoned when the Chinese government refused it entry. Both were peace projects that bore 'witness' to pacifist values, rather than the major acts of nonviolent intervention that the WPB founders had originally envisaged. In the context of liberation struggles, proposals for the nonviolent invasion of South Africa and also Namibia, whose cause Michael Scott championed, were not taken up. After the WPB's expiry, a similar fate befell Ralph Bell's proposal that the British government should respond to Southern Rhodesia's Unilateral Declaration of Independence in 1965 by organising a Commonwealth nonviolent expeditionary force (*Peace News* 19 August 1966). The idea of nonviolent action at the transnational level — organised by pacifists rather than by governments! — did not die with the WPB, as shown by the 1968 project for Nonviolent Action in Vietnam, intended to send medical orderlies into North Vietnam (see *Peace News* 29 March 1968), and Operation Omega, which succeeded in entering Bangladesh in 1971. In 1981, the Peace Brigades International was formed, a contingent of which is presently working in Central America. But, clearly, the high hopes entertained by the founders of WPB have not been realised.

In retrospect, it is evident that, by the time the WBP was formed, the Gandhian model for national liberation was already ceasing to attract African leaders. They were turning to another model with a different technique: that provided in China by

Everyman III at Gravesend before sailing to Leningrad in 1961.

Mao. The technique of guerrilla warfare, so it seemed to them, was the appropriate one to use wherever colonial regimes were unresponsive to constitutional or nonviolent action — the situation in Algeria, in Portugal's African colonies, in Southern Rhodesia, and in South Africa. In the latter country, where the white settler regime had bolstered its rule with the system of apartheid, the African National Congress (ANC) had experimented with 'Gandhian techniques' from 1920 onwards. In 1953, led by Luthuli, it had conducted a major civil disobedience Campaign in Defiance of Unjust Laws. It had been harshly and successfully crushed. Then, in 1960, occurred the Sharpeville Massacre. For the ANC, this marked the turning point and provided the justification for adopting a new policy of selective sabotage as a build up to guerrilla warfare. Nelson Mandela, an exponent of this policy, emerged as the principal leader of his people, a position which his detention since 1963 has served only to strengthen and which, in 1986, is not questioned even by those, such as Bishop Desmond Tutu and Dr Allan Boesak, who continue to advocate nonviolent resistance.

The ANC's new policy prompted Gene Sharp, the indefatigable exponent and leading theorist of nonviolent action, to publish in *Peace News* an article 'Can nonviolence work in South Africa?'[18] He argued that, in spite of the difficulties, it could and that, in terms of human suffering, continued nonviolent resistance would prove less costly than guerrilla warfare. The latter he predicted — rightly, as it turned out — would also be difficult to organise, and would provide the excuse for even harsher repression. To cite Sharpeville as justification for abandoning nonviolent action showed a grave misunderstanding of the dynamics of the technique. It was precisely because unarmed demonstrators had been murdered that such deep feelings had been aroused in South Africa and around the world. It was naive to believe that by using nonviolent action one could avoid suffering and escape repression. In South Africa, there had not been enough nonviolent action and it had been used too sporadically. The apartheid regime, like all regimes, depended on the co-operation of the majority of the population. Withdrawal of that co-operation was necessary. Guerrilla movements, too, recognised this, which was why they so often directed terror against their own people, to force them into resistance, rather than against the 'enemy'. Sharp also pointed out that violent struggles, unlike nonviolent ones, tend to concentrate power in the hands of those who control the means of violence and thus lead to replacing one dominating minority by another. This was an important consideration if one was really concerned with liberation.

Sharp's skilful presentation of the case for nonviolent action, later elaborated in *The Politics of Nonviolent Action*, 1973, did not, of course, deflect the turn towards violent action in South Africa and in Third World countries generally. It also did not persuade some *Peace News* readers who abandoned their pacifism when they came to the conclusion that in many Third World countries nonviolent action offered no practical alternative to armed struggle.[19] Those who remained pacifists, however, have continued to deploy Sharp's arguments whenever the debate is over armed versus unarmed struggle. But the debate is not always posed in such simple terms. As the current rebellion in South Africa illustrates, the issue for liberation movements is not between violent and nonviolent action: it is whether to rely *exclusively* on the latter. The ANC and other anti-apartheid organisations not only advocate further application of non-violent sanctions on South Africa from outside, but also use a variety of nonviolent methods within the country. These methods — school and consumer boycotts, the holding of illegal demonstrations, strikes and so on — are often accompanied by spontaneous violence and terroristic acts directed against the police and black collaborators. The movement thus counters the growing violence of the South African state with both violence and nonviolence. From the perspective which presents nonviolent action as a technique, to be adopted on pragmatic rather than principled grounds, it is not immediately obvious that a 'pure' strategy of nonviolence is superior to a 'mixed' strategy. When the going gets rough or the objective sought is not speedily achieved, a 'pure' strategy is likely to be adhered to only by those with a principled commitment to nonviolence. Here it is relevant to note that, although Gandhi advocated satyagraha on the ground that, in the long run at least, it would always be effective, he attributed any failures, not to the technique but to the weaknesses of those, including himself, who used it. *By definition*, satyagraha could not fail; only its practitioners could do so. Fundamentally, for him satyagraha was not susceptible to empirical disproof; it was an expression of a philosophy of life.

For pacifists, too, nonviolent action is really rooted in a philosophy of life. This became increasingly clear as they moved, in the mid-Sixties, into the third phase, when 'nonviolent revolution' becomes the predominant orientation. The provenance of this concept is, of course, Gandhian, and its adoption signals a growing appreciation that other aspects of Gandhi's message besides his way of fighting are relevant to pacifism. Gandhi's idea that nonviolent revolution is not a programme for the seizure of power but a programme for the transformation of relationships is, perhaps, the central notion that pacifism in this phase derives from him. It implies taking nonviolence seriously, regarding it as something more than the absence of violent behaviour, and asking, as in effect Gandhi had done: What are the essential conditions that must be met if there is ever to be a nonviolent society and world?

In the preceding phase, when pacifists were promoting nonviolent action as a technique, the framework of their thinking, even for most socialists among them, remained essentially liberal-democratic. There was inadequate appreciation that pacifism involves profound changes in the way society is presently organised; and the technique is defined largely in behavioural terms. There was no firm grasp of the concept of 'structural violence', the idea that social structures — sets of relationships that have persisted through time — may harm people, just as overt violent behaviour does. Those on the wrong end of many relationships may suffer poverty, famine, disease, and premature death. Gandhi himself did not use the term 'structural violence', but he clearly understood that many relationships involve covert violence that is no less objectionable than overt violence.

'Structural violence', however, is a concept shared by many revolutionaries, and it is likely that, when pacifists became nonviolent revolutionaries, they derived it less from Gandhism than from Marxism and anarchism which were the more obvious ideological influences on the New Left. The concept is often invoked by revolutionaries to justify the use of overt violence by, or on behalf of, the oppressed. Nonviolent revolutionaries, of course, do not invoke it thus, but their appreciation of the pervasiveness of structural violence has tempered the 'absolute' quality of their pacifism and made them less moralistic. They have come to accept that spontaneous violence of the oppressed is a natural human reaction which it is pointless to moralise about. And they have become less inclined to pass judgement on those, who, when they feel that no alternative is available to them, resist oppression by violent means. As pacifists, they draw the line at taking part themselves in organised violence, but they do not equate the violence of the oppressed with that of their oppressors. In this respect, their position is similar to Gandhi's: provided it is not barbaric, violent resistance to injustice is always preferable to passive acquiescence for cowardly reasons.

The New Left of the late Fifties and early Sixties, of which radical pacifism became one element, was triggered off by disillusionment with Soviet Marxism. At the same time, it was highly critical of Democratic Socialism, which seemed incapable of moving beyond the capitalist Welfare-cum-Warfare State. In terms of the Cold War, both superpowers and their respective allies, and what they represented, stood condemned. In this context, there was a notable revival and rediscovery of ideas associated with the then dormant tradition of libertarian socialism. At the centre of this tradition had been anarchism, which accepted much of the Marxist critique of capitalism but, unlike Marxism, insisted that the structures of capitalism were integrally linked with those of the modern state. Anarchists argued, therefore, that socialists should not take over the state but abolish it in the course of the revolution. Direct action, as opposed to party and parliamentary action, was the classical anarchist mode. So when radical nuclear disarmers adopted it to confront the state, anarchists joined them. Ideas were exchanged and in the process anarcho-pacifism began to take more definite shape. The failure of nuclear disarmers, evident by 1965, to shift the policy of the state on the issue of 'the Bomb', and the state's repressive response to their actions, helped to impel pacifists in an anarchist direction.[20] They began to realise that 'the Bomb' is more than a horrendous instrument of mass destruction: it is the end-product of organised violence in the shape of the state, and a symbol of all that is rotten in modern society. To get rid of it, state and society had to be radically changed.

As New Left movements progressed through the Sixties before disintegrating and fragmenting in the early Seventies, old habits of thought and old structures were increasingly challenged. Liberation became the new watchword. (For example, when Michael Randle drafted the WRI statement in 1975, it was called

Towards Liberation.) A new revolutionary consciousness appeared to be emerging, heralding the end of oppression, the transformation of people's lives and their relationships with one another and with the world. A notable element in the new consciousness was an increased awareness of the oneness of humanity: a realisation that, although human beings are divided in countless different ways, they share a common fate and live in a single world. Those with this awareness tend naturally to link their own struggle for liberation with struggles of people elsewhere. This is true of both violent and nonviolent revolutionaries.

Among the many factors contributing to the growth in recent decades of a global consciousness, one has been the spread of Marxism, an ideology some variant of which has come to be held by most violent revolutionaries. According to this ideology, as developed by Lenin and his successors, the twentieth century is the epoch of imperialism which is also, in its later stage, the epoch of transition to a socialist world. Capitalism, which developed first in Europe and then the USA, has become a worldwide system, characterised by a division of labour between exploiting and exploited countries. The relationship is structural and initially took the form in which, typically, the exploiting 'bourgeois' countries exercised overt political domination over the exploited 'proletarian' countries. In the latter, the colonial and semi-colonial countries, nationalist movements are generated. But, unless such movements are led by Marxist parties and become movements for both national and socialist liberation, they do not lead to the liquidation of imperialism. The mere achievement of political independence signifies little — ex-colonies simply become 'neo-colonies', alongside other nominally independent countries in a similar position. The developed capitalist countries continue to exploit the undeveloped ones in various ways — through aid, loans, investments by multi-national companies — and thus maintain the dependent relationship. In undeveloped countries where socialist revolution threatens the relationship, capitalist countries, headed by the USA, actively intervene to bolster right-wing regimes and military dictatorships.

Much of this Marxist picture of the world is acceptable to nonviolent revolutionaries. But they do not accept the political conclusions Marxists draw from their analysis, their strategy of revolution, or their notion that industrialisation provides the key to development. Marx's observation that 'The country that is more developed industrially only shows the less developed the image if its own future', reflects his view that industrial capitalism provides the basis for the advance to socialism. As it has turned out, Marxist revolutions have taken place, not in 'the more developed' but in 'the less developed', predominantly peasant, countries. But, having captured political power, Marxist revolutionaries then pursue a policy of industrialisation. In doing so, they are, in a sense, upholding Marx's belief that industrialisation is progressive, but adding that in their case it is proceeding under socialist, rather than capitalist, direction. Not all Marxist regimes have pursued industrialisation so rigorously and with such a lop-sided emphasis on heavy industry as did the Soviet Union under Stalin. Mao, for one, did not. After the Sino-Soviet split, the Maoist development strategy included more emphasis on small and medium scale enterprises, rural industrialisation, the organisation of peasants in communes, national self-sufficiency and self-reliance — items with a Gandhian flavour to them. But investment in heavy industry remained high, and the goal, which his revisionist successors have continued to pursue, remains unchanged: a modern industrial nation state. Given that this (and not the Communist stateless utopia) is the goal, the Marxist and capitalist development strategies are only different ways to the same end.

Since pacifists in becoming nonviolent revolutionaries rejected this end, they came to look more closely at those who were pursuing a genuinely alternative development strategy. Foremost among them were 'the village revolutionaries' of India's Sarvodaya movement. Writing about them in *Peace News* (6 June 1967), Bjorn Merker observed that the axis of conflict in the world had swung from an East-West to a North-South position. 'Development' was defined as movement towards Western social patterns, Western economic and political models, with the help of Western theories and often under the supervision of Western experts, with Western capital and foreign aid. And an 'undeveloped country' was defined as one which had not yet succeeded in copying Western production and social patterns, or acknowledged the superiority of Western values and goals. It was not surprising that in many 'undeveloped countries', the masses did not respond positively to the imported development plans designed by their Westernised elites. Their implementation had widened the gap between the rich elites and the impoverished masses because poor countries had no areas to exploit other than their own countryside which served the role of a colonial territory. The Sarvodaya movement had the wisdom to question, and mostly discard as irrelevant, present Western modes of thought about progress. It was staking its revolution on the peasants and the ability of villages to plan and provide for their own needs.

Pacifists also looked sympathetically, if critically, at Nyerere's attempt to pursue an alternative path of development in Tanzania where, after 'The Arusha Declaration' of 1967, the policy was to establish 'village socialism' through the *ujamaa* scheme. *Peace News* (8 May 1970) quoted approvingly Nyerere's words: 'Development means the development of people. But people cannot be developed; they can only develop themselves.'

But perhaps the most important influence in these years on the thinking of pacifists, and many others, about development came from the writings of E F Schumacher, following his visit to India in 1961.[21] In countries such as India, where capital is scarce and labour abundant, what is needed, he argued, is not large-scale industry, using the latest technology, but 'intermediate technology', the central features of which are: 'simplicity, cheapness, smallness and nonviolence.' It encourages economic growth, but of a form which leads back to the real needs of people; this also means taking account of their actual size. Instead of the destructive and ecologically violent system of mass production, Schumacher advocated 'a technology by the masses' which is 'conducive to decentralisation, compatible with the laws of ecology, gentle in its use of scarce resources, and designed to serve the human person instead of making him the servant of machines.' In essence, he restated, in a more accessible form, important insights of Gandhi.

Schumacher's ideas, although stimulated by thinking about problems of development in the Third World, had clear relevance to industrial societies of the First and Second Worlds. The latter, as increasing numbers of people, especially the young, came to see in the late Sixties, had developed in the wrong direction and become 'over-developed'. This view was most strongly held by those New Leftists who began to elaborate the notion of 'counter-culture' and, later, the concept of 'the alternative society'. Central to the counter-culture was its radical critique of modern industrial civilisation and the materialist values it generates. The critique was expounded impressively in a series of books by the American, Theodore Roszak, who edited *Peace News*, 1964–65.[22]

However, only some New Leftists moved in the direction of 'counter-culture', 'the alternative society', and nonviolent revolution. Others, mainly Trotskyists and Maoists, were attracted to the idea of 'revolutionary violence' which had found new defenders in Fanon, Sartre and Marcuse. They saw wars of liberation in the Third World as attacks on the imperialist heartland, Amerika, and as surrogates, or even models, for the revolution at home. For them, as for almost everybody, the war in Vietnam became a major issue. For pacifists, the war was of special concern, because in South Vietnam Buddhists, through nonviolent action, including self-immolation by monks, had been largely instrumental in the overthrow in 1964 of the Diem dictatorship, which was then replaced by another US-backed dictatorship. The Buddhists stood for a 'third way' of resolving the conflict and, although relatively weak, they attempted not only to stop the war but also to develop a movement for nonviolent revolution. As the vicious war dragged on, the conflict polarised sharply. Opinion outside Vietnam also became polarised, and there was a marked tendency in Western peace movements, even among pacifists, to side with the National Liberation Front. The NLF were seen as fighting for the liberation of the Vietnamese people and, if pacifists could not support the military struggle, they should, some argued, support the NLF's aims.

It was in this context that Nigel Young wrote articles for *Peace News* which formed the basis of a pamphlet, *On War, National Liberation and the State*, 1971.[23] This cogently argued statement has greatly influenced the thinking of nonviolent revolutionaries, presents clearly their general position on the issues, and remains of continuing relevance.

Pre-war pacifism, Young observes, had stressed the ethical relationship between ends and means but had not usually included a critique of the structural relationship between the two. Bart de Ligt had been a notable exception and, more recently, in the context of the Cuban revolution, Mulford Sibley had restated and elaborated de Ligt's point: 'The greater the violence, other things being equal, the less the revolution.'[24]

Developing his thesis that ends and means are structurally inseparable, Young points out that wars of national liberation are (i) *wars*, that is, collective, hierarchically organised violence;

(ii) *nationalist*, even when combined with a Marxist ideology; and (iii) they liberate *forces* rather than *people*. Modern war is inextricably linked with the process of building states; and wars of national liberation are no different in this respect. Those who wage them are engaged in the same process:

> mobilising and centralising men and resources, centralising communication, creating new kinds of top-down political structures . . . that support this mobilisation, and a modern 'people's' army, with a nationalist ideology — and ultimately rapid industrialisation geared to this military expansion. Revolutionary war is consciously chosen as a means of achieving these organisational ends.

Many Third World leaders may say that they wish to avoid Western or Soviet models of development. But, substantially, they accept the model of progress which makes a fetish of industrial production and modern political structures. Industrialisation and modernisation develop in relation to changes in the rural sector — extraction of the surplus through taxes and requisitions, the commercialisation or collectivisation of agriculture, and the urbanisation of peasants. The changes break up the existing peasant order, and the peasants tend to resist, using spontaneous violence and non-co-operation. Peasants do not want industrialisation. They want land, bread, and peace. But they become the principal victims of modernisation.

'Wars of national liberation', Young insists, 'represent the elite-led, mass-organised violence which mobilises sections of peasant societies in the interests of modernisation, state-building and industrialisation.' Since pacifists share neither the means nor the inseparable ends, they should not choose sides in such wars on the ground that they are 'anti-imperialist'.

What, then, should pacifists do? They should seek to prevent the export of arms to the Third World. They should try to inhibit the export of Western models and ideas, whether capitalist or Marxist, and be prepared, for a change, to learn from non-Western societies. And, recognising that our own societies stand in an oppressive relationship with Third World societies, they should develop nonviolent strategies which specify the relationship, alleviate the pressures, and, through revolutionary change, destroy the oppression. But, ultimately, concludes Young, 'our prime task is to make our own revolution — nonviolently.'

The conclusion is one that accords well with Gandhi's

interpretation of the *swadeshi* spirit. Fifteen years further on, that is still the prime task. And for the next fifty years and beyond, it will remain so for those whose programme is, like Gandhi's, not the seizure of power but the transformation of all relationships in accordance with the principle of nonviolence.

Acknowledgement. I wish to thank Bill Hetherington and Diana Shelley for helpful comments on the draft of this chapter.

1. M K Gandhi, *Village Swaraj*, Ahmedabad, 1963, p. 14.
2. ibid., p. 16.
3. M K Gandhi, *The Constructive Programme*, rev. edn., Ahmedabad, 1945. Among the items is achieving equality of status and opportunity for women.
4. N K Bose, *Selections from Gandhi*, Ahmedabad, 1957, p. 41.
5. Quoted in R Bideleux, *Communism and Development*, 1985, p. 48.
6. For an account of the movement, see my *Nonviolent Revolution in India*, Gandhi Peace Foundation, New Delhi/Housmans, London, 1985.
7. For the contrast between 'conventional' and 'alternative' development strategies, see R K Diwan & D Lingston, *Alternative Development Strategies and Appropriate Technology*, New York, 1979.
8. *The Guardian*, 16 August 1985.
9. See Albert Beale, *Against All War: Fifty Years of Peace News*, 1986.
10. M K Gandhi, *For Pacifists*, Ahmedabad, 1949, pp v–vii.
11. D Sheppard, *I Will Not Fight*, originally published 1937, republished by PPU, 1985.
12. For example, Aldous Huxley, *Pacifism and Philosophy*, 1936, republished by PPU, 1985. See also his *Ends and Means*, 1937, and Ronald Duncan, *The Complete Pacifist*, 1937.
13. B de Ligt, *The Conquest of Violence*, 1937. The English edition carried an introduction by Aldous Huxley.
14. A Huxley, *The Case for Constructive Peace*, 1936, republished by PPU, 1984. Bill Hetherington is, therefore, correct in stating that 'The ideas of Gandhi were permeating the (PPU) movement from the beginning.' He adds, 'and they strengthened with time.' Bill Hetherington, *Resisting War*, PPU, 1986, p. 17.
15. A Mazrui, *Political Values and the Educated Class in Africa*, 1978, ch. 5.
16. *Ghana, The Autobiography of Kwame Nkrumah*, 1957, p. 92.
17. For an account of the WPB, see C Walker in A P Hare & H H Blumberg (eds) *Liberation Without Violence*, 1977, and Theodore Olson in *Peace News*, 25 September 1964. The various pacifist and nonviolent initiatives should not be confused with the Peace Corps, a form of overseas service for young people sponsored by the American government and mistrusted by many in the receiving countries.
18. *Peace News*, 21 & 28 June & 5 July 1963. A revised version has been published as ch. 7 of his book, *Social Power and Political Freedom*, 1980.
19. See, for example, the letter on Third World Revolution from Aidan Foster-Carter in *Peace News*, 13 October 1967, and the subsequent correspondence on the issue.

20. A notable indication of this was the publication in 1970 of Ronald Sampson's *The Anarchist Basis of Pacifism*, republished as *Society Without the State*, 3rd ed., PPU, 1986. Earlier, an editorial in *Peace News*, 5 January 1968, stated that 'The pacifism of *Peace News* is very close to anarchism these days . . . .'
21. The more important of these writings, originally published in 'alternative' journals, notably *Resurgence*, formed the basis of his best-seller, *Small is Beautiful*, 1973. See also his article in *Peace News*, 20 January 1966.
22. *The Making of a Counter Culture*, 1969; *Where the Wasteland Ends*, 1972; *Unfinished Animal* 1976; and *Person/Planet*, 1979.
23. *Peace News*, 21 November 1969 and 8 January 1971. See also the Appendix in his book, *An Infantile Disorder? The Crisis and Decline of the New Left*, 1977.
24. M Sibley, *Revolution and Violence*, Housmans, 1959; reprinted in *Peace News*, 30 April 1965.

Afterword

by Petra Karin Kelly

I congratulate *Peace News* on its 50th anniversary. I feel honoured to be able to write the afterword for this book marking 50 years of continuous pacifist publication.

This book covers an important range of subjects which have relevance not only in Great Britain, but all over Europe, all over the world. Pacifism and war resistance, as well as nonviolent resistance and social defence, alternative lifestyles and feminism and nonviolence are issues which are interconnected and which are the motivating factors for many of the social movements all over Western Europe. I also feel that we need to do much more concrete thinking about the Gandhian alternative, about liberation and development. And this book is a beginning in the right direction. As Albert Einstein once said, 'Mere praise of peace is simple, but ineffective. What we need is active participation in the struggle against war and everything that leads to war.'

The arms build-up on every level, whether nuclear, chemical, conventional or even biological has continued, at painful cost to the world community. Ruth Leger Sivard, in her publication, *World Military and Social Expenditures 1985*, describes current political priorities, which are of a military and not social nature. The megatonnage in the world's stockpile of nuclear weapons is enough to kill 58 billion people — to kill every person now living 12 times. In the Third World, military spending has increased fivefold since 1960 and the number of countries ruled by military governments has grown from 22 to 57. The USA and USSR, first in military power, rank 14 and 51 among all nations in their infant mortality rates. The budget of the US Airforce is larger than the total educational budget for 1.2 billion children in Africa, Latin America and Asia, excluding Japan. The Soviet Union spends more in one year on military defence than the governments of all the developing countries spend for education and health care for 3.6 billion people. There is one soldier per 43 people in the world, and one physician for 1030 people. Only one citizen in four in developing countries has an unrestricted right to vote. It costs US $590,000 a day to operate one aircraft carrier, and yet every day, in Africa alone, 14,000 children die of hunger or hunger-related causes.

When looking at this order of priorities, it is most urgent to begin exploring concrete alternatives to the build-up of military force and to look into the idea of deterrent philosophy. World security is at present at a most critical stage. After the tragic disaster at Chernobyl, after the announcement of the Secretary of Defense, Caspar Weinberger, that the United States will no longer respect SALT II limits, after repeated nuclear tests in the Pacific and in Nevada by both the French and the United States governments, while the terrible interventions go on in Central America and a cruel war is raging in Afghanistan, we must scream loud and clear, in order to be heard. And usually, nonviolent actions and campaigns speak much louder than any words. In recent years, the two superpowers have sat down to negotiate arms controls over the most dangerous elements of the arms race, but we all realise that positive results are hardly on the way, and that while negotiations go on, new and more precise, more dangerous weapons systems are being created every single day.

On the other hand, there have been some breakthroughs, when one considers New Zealand's comprehensive nuclear-free stance, which includes a ban on entry into its ports of nuclear armed ships. The New Zealand public campaign for Nuclear Free Zones has been one of the roots of New Zealand's success. As of spring 1985, over 65% of New Zealanders lived in 94 locally declared Nuclear Free Zones, a world record in terms of the proportion of the population covered. Another break-through has been the Soviet declaration to stop nuclear testing on August 6 (Hiroshima Day) 1985 and its decision to extend this unilateral moratorium until August 6, 1986. But will the United States ever think of following? And there has been a most hopeful growth of feminist, Third World, anti-nuclear and peace movement initiatives around the world. Finally, we are joining up again, linking arms together as people committed in the struggle against both the civilian and the military uses of nuclear energy. They cannot be separated, they are Siamese twins, and we must make sure that the ecological and peace movements act united on these issues.

In a world scarred by violence and poverty, the Star War Programme continues, the Europeans plan on expanding their EUREKA projects, there are plans not only for a Strategic Defence Initiative, but also for a European Defence Initiative, and some of our right-wing politicians in Western Europe dream of a united nuclear superpower called Europe (or United States of Europe), with a joint British and French nuclear potential which will eventually be available to the Federal Republic of Germany, so that Germany would then also have its finger on the trigger.

The question constantly remains: why is it not possible for the superpowers and other countries, like Great Britain, France and Germany to announce that they will make billions of dollars a year available for unprecedented human development programmes instead of military programmes? There is so much to do in the world: training programmes for young handicapped people, literacy drives emphasising skills for women, health care networks for women, children and elderly people, labourintensive, medium-term ecological technology in decentralised, safe and healthy energy systems, safe water and sanitation for all, community-based health services, new schools and teacher training, nutrients to supplement foods, development of organic farming. The list is almost endless.

The gap between education and military budgets is actually widest in the developing countries. In these countries, in 1982, military expenditures per soldier averaged US $9810, while educational expenditures per head of population reached only US $32, and only 50% of children attended school. We have all the statistics and all the analysis about the growing gap between poor and rich, about social underdevelopment, and unemployment, the lack of food and the lack of health and educational services. And yet our governments seem unable to solve any of these problems and, in fact, act criminally by continuing to produce nuclear weapons and so-called peaceful nuclear energy. Nuclear research and an expanding commercial nuclear power industry for producing electricity have brought nuclear reactors to 56 countries. There are now over 500 nuclear power plants operating. And since Chernobyl we know that Chernobyl is everywhere. There is no peaceful nuclear energy.

Meanwhile, the peace-making expenditure of the United

Nations is, in comparison with military expenditure, so minute as to be barely visible. More than anything else we need conflict resolution, non-military forms of defence (social defence) and civil disobedience campaigns, following the Gandhian way.

A number of people in the peace movement, including myself, have come to feel that the interior dimension of people searching for peace is often being overlooked. As we once thought of the physical world as separate bodies, acting on one another primarily by collision, so we thought of the social world, too, as changed only by coercive forces. Many of our resources have to do with our own daily life, with the way in which we live, with the way in which we change ourselves. The tradition within the peace movement of seeking to live one's politics and attempting to move one's life into closer accord with the values of non-exploitation, liberation, freedom, equality and mutual aid are the most important elements in disarming and in creating peace around us. As Storm Jameson, a British essayist, wrote: 'All of us wish for peace, but we do not will it.' I believe that the Peace Movement and the other social movements all have a spiritual dimension. The depth of our own change cannot happen in one single day, this change must be renewed every day and continue all the rest of our life.

We are looking for a new power, power shared with others, not power exercised to gain control over them. Feminism, ecology and nonviolence belong together and are interrelated. But at the same time, we must be watchful that, while we struggle together against the big war, the little war in our everyday life is not forgotten — the little war being raged against the weak, the handicapped, the elderly, against children and women. All of us must be concerned with both levels: the big and the little war waged against us as individuals, against smaller countries, against the planetary environment, every single day. Resistance to war, to the use of nuclear weapons and nuclear energy is impossible without resistance to sexism, to racism, to imperialism and to violence as an everyday pervasive reality. There is a very profound relationship between the fact that many women and children are commonly attacked, beaten up and raped, and that a nuclear war as well as a nuclear catastrophe threatens this entire planet Earth, which has no emergency exit.

Present technology within the patriarchal system had made it possible to create first-strike missiles like Pershing II, which can reach the Soviet Union within 6 minutes. Yet those very same patriarchal societies have not been able to solve the most urgent problems and the most basic needs in many parts of the world. Women in Asia, Africa and Latin America must still fetch water from far away, carrying weights up to 20 kilos at a time, and this can take up to 5 hours every day.

We can no longer separate ourselves from the suffering and the wisdom of our sisters and brothers in Asia, Africa, and Latin America, in Australia and New Zealand and in other parts of the world. There can be no true peace, there can be no respect for human rights and justice, while one race dominates another, one people, one nation, one sex, despises the other.

This book is about new forms of power, not about power over, or about domination, terrorising and oppression. It is about a new power called nonviolence and civil disobedience, about abolishing power as we have known it and redefining power as something common to all, to be used by all and for all. Patriarchal power is to be replaced by shared power, by the discovery of our own strength, as opposed to a passive receiving of power exercised by others, often in our name.

And so we must, all of us, women and men of a peaceful nature across the world, begin moving together, towards the doors of the nuclear and chemical and conventional weapons laboratories, towards the doors of the weapons factories and the nuclear power plants, towards the doors of the men (and Mrs Thatcher) in power. Towards the doors of military alliances, towards the doors of those who tread upon human rights, towards the doors of those who oppress and discriminate. And as we sit and blockade those doors, we must begin our silent meditations and our hopeful songs and our conversations among ourselves, so that we can feel energised and strong and no longer alone. Then the distance between our convictions and the limits of our daily lives ceases to exist. What else is there to do than to practise civil disobedience and active nonviolence in our daily lives at a time when US $1,300,000 are spent every minute on the arms race? We have never before been so endangered. We must call upon people all over the world to renew their forces in a nonviolent effort of resistance and civil disobedience. We must convince the old, established authorities that a new enlightened authority exists — the power of reason and love, the power of communal awareness and nonviolence.

Peace News was launched on June 6, 1936 to serve the growing pacifist movement of that era. It survived the war it steadfastly opposed and since then has reported on numerous campaigns—such as the start of CND in 1958 through the Biafran famine in the 60s to the movement against nuclear power in the 70s, all of which it was a major force behind.

In the 80s *Peace News* reflects its involvement in those and other campaigns—there's coverage of nuclear disarmament, ecology, feminism, nonviolence, animal rights, conscientious objection . . .

Every fortnight—the independent peace reporting you can't afford to miss!

1936~1986

SUBSCRIBE!

Peace News was launched on June 6, 1936 to serve the growing pacifist movement of that era. It survived the war it steadfastly opposed and since then has reported on numerous campaigns—such as the start of CND in 1958 through the Biafran famine in the 60s to the movement against nuclear power in the 70s, all of which it was a major force behind.

In the 80s *Peace News* reflects its involvement in those and other campaigns—there's coverage of nuclear disarmament, ecology, feminism, nonviolence, animal rights, conscientious objection . . .

Every fortnight—the independent peace reporting you can't afford to miss!

1936~1986

SUBSCRIBE!

Inland

One year	£12	☐
Six months	£6.50	☐
Trial sub (5 issues	£2.50	☐

Supporter (includes all pamphlets produced in the year) £25 ☐

Overseas
Surface (worldwide)

one year	£14	☐
six months	£7.50	☐

Airmail Europe

one year	£15	☐
six months	£8	☐

Airmail rest of world

one year	£17	☐
six months	£9	☐

10% discount for all unwaged subscribers *except* trial subscriptions. Payments from overseas should be made in £ Sterling, otherwise, add £1 to cover bank charges.

Name . . . .
Address. . . . .
. . . .
. . . .

Peace News, 8 Elm Avenue, Nottingham NG3 4GF

Or order *Peace News* through your local newsagent now!

FORTNIGHTLY ON FRIDAYS   **50p**